ART AND LIFE IN AFRICA

ART AND LIFE IN AFRICA

Selections from the Stanley Collection, Exhibitions of 1985 and 1992

Christopher D. Roy

THE UNIVERSITY OF IOWA MUSEUM OF ART
Distributed by The University of Washington Press

Photography:

Field photographs by Christopher Roy

Cat. no. 84 from the Catalogue of the 1985 Exhibition (black and white) by Thomas Drew

Other black and white photographs from the Catalogue of the 1985
    Exhibition by Steve Tatum

Cat. nos. 34, 78, 79, 93, 97, 105, 108, 109, and 114 (color) from the
    Catalogue of the 1985 Exhibition by Randall Tosh

Other color photographs from the Catalogue of the 1985 Exhibition by Richard Beaulieux

Photograph of Max Stanley by Bachrach Studios

Photograph of Elizabeth Stanley by Jon Van Allen

All photographs from the Catalogue of the 1992 Exhibition by Mark Tade, Iowa City, Iowa

Front cover photo: Cat. 26 from the Catalogue of the 1992 Exhibition

Back cover photo: Cat. 24 from the Catalogue of the 1992 Exhibition

Frontispiece: Cat. 125 from the Catalogue of the 1985 Exhibition

Design: Kachergis Book Design, Pittsboro, North Carolina

Printing and Binding: Toppan Printing Company, Inc., Japan

CONTENTS

MAX AND BETTY STANLEY

FOREWORD

We have finally gotten over the turn-of-the-century French fashion of viewing African art as a manifestation of the eternal mystery of life and have begun to look at this art as representative of distinct cultures, as meaningful in context. Although their strange allure still enchants and intrigues us, we are now beginning to look at these sculptures as less denizens of an eternal psychological realm and more art created out of the secular and spiritual needs of distinct peoples in Africa.

The exhibition and book, *Art and Life in Africa: The Stanley Collection*, represents a remarkable collaboration between two Iowa collectors, Mr. and Mrs. C. Maxwell Stanley, and one scholar, Professor Christopher Roy. The collectors have been intrigued with the mysterious qualities and the subtle refinements of these sculptures which at first appeared to them to be enormously abstract, and the scholar began his investigation of African life with his wife, Nora, when the two of them spent time in Africa as Peace Corps volunteers. Both the Stanleys and Chris Roy have worked diligently over the past six years to put together one of the more remarkable collections in this country. Respectful of the fact that their collection would eventually be given to The University of Iowa Museum of Art

where it would be integral to an African studies program, Max and Betty Stanley listened and responded to Chris's defense of certain tribes' works and of his concern with filling in gaps. The collection is balanced, and it is grounded in a desire to familiarize students with the wealth and variety of types of African art. And it is also based on intense discussions and on occasion after occasion when both the collectors and the scholar were seduced by the sheer beauty and intensity of powerfully conceived forms.

I believe that the collection has benefited from this dialogue, and the exhibition, *Art and Life in Africa*, represents the fruits of this exploration, this pursuit of quality and also of historical understanding.

We of The University of Iowa Museum of Art are greatly indebted to Max and Betty Stanley and also to Chris Roy for putting together such a remarkable collection, and we are particularly pleased that the Stanleys have wanted their collection to be permanently housed in this museum. It's indeed a privilege to be able to share part of this important collection with the University community and the general public in the form of this catalogue which the Stanleys have so generously provided.

Robert C. Hobbs, *Director, The University of Iowa Museum of Art,* 1984

This edition of *Art and Life in Africa* is a revised and expanded version of the catalogue published in 1985. In the years following Max Stanley's death in 1984, Betty Stanley acquired 134 additional objects, and a selection of those acquisitions has been incorporated here into the original catalogue. Betty Stanley passed away in the spring of 1990, and this new edition is intended to document in a final, comprehensive manner the wonderful collection the Stanleys have given to The University of Iowa.

We have retained the original organization of the 1985 catalogue, and have added the objects Betty purchased following the same geographical plan. The advantage of delimiting broad style areas according to major physical features, especially river systems, is that it gives both readers and teachers who use the catalogues as texts greater freedom to select objects or groups of objects for study in any order they choose, and to structure their own study of the collection after their own particular approach. Although a geographical plan is clearly only one of several options available, I am gratified that increasing numbers of scholars have agreed that rivers and other major geographical features are useful in defining style areas.

A number of constraints have limited the number of new objects in this edition to 177. Together with *African Sculpture: The Stanley Collection*, it represents most of the outstanding objects acquired by Max and Betty, but still less than half of the total collection. A catalogue of multiple views of the entire collection is available on videodisk from The Office of Visual Materials, The School of Art and Art History, The University of Iowa.

Christopher D. Roy, *Curator of African, Oceanic, and New-World Cultures, The University of Iowa Museum of Art; Associate Professor of Art History, The University of Iowa School of Art and Art History,* 1991

ACKNOWLEDGMENTS

Since late spring, 1981, when Max and Betty and I first began to plan this exhibition of the Stanley Collection, many people here at Iowa and in Europe and the United States have helped with advice, connoisseurship, and scholarship. Dealers have sought out objects that would improve the quality of the collection, scholars have helped to identify the origins, use, function, and meaning of the objects, and the staff at The University of Iowa Museum of Art has assisted with photography, organization and design of the catalogue, research, and the mounting of the exhibition. I would like to thank everyone who has helped us so generously.

The beautiful color photographs were made by Dick Beaulieux, who travelled all the way from Brussels, and Randall Tosh, who also photographed the Vuvi mask for the exhibition poster. Steven Tatum, who is currently studying Luba sculpture, made all of the black and white photographs.

The task of organizing photographs, keeping track of objects in Iowa City and Muscatine, and creating research files has been skillfully handled by the museum registrar, Jo-Ann Conklin, and by the assistant registrar, Jean Schroeder. I would like to thank them especially for being patient with my frequent demands for photographs on 24-hours notice. Claire Kuennen-Jordan sent letters requesting expertise to scholars all over the world, and gathered great quantities of recently published scholarship for the catalogue entries. The organization of the final stages of the catalogue research and production, and the task of keeping things on schedule during my spring research trip to Burkina Faso, has been the responsibility of Karen Hueftle.

The superb installation of the exhibition is the work of David Dennis, Installation Coordinator, and his assistant James Lindell. Numerous Iowa students have lent a hand as museum technicians.

Robert Hobbs, Director of The University of Iowa Museum of Art, and Judith McTammany, Administrative Assistant, have helped with organization, funding, installation, and coordination. During the past six years' work on the Stanley Collection, Nancy DeDakis has provided invaluable assistance on many tasks.

The text was edited carefully and with great restraint by Jennifer Atkinson, a graduate student in the Department of English.

The beautiful catalogue design is the work of Ann Walston, of the firm of Joyce Kachergis Book Design and Production, Bynum, North Carolina.

An enormously important contribution has been made to the exhibition by the many scholars who have responded to my requests for assistance in identifying tribal styles and describing the role objects play in the lives of the people who made and used them. Scholars in Europe, America, and Africa have been selfless in their willingness to share the results of their field research, making the catalogue a useful document rather than just a perfunctory record of this wonderful collection. This willingness to share knowledge has been a consistent virtue of the prominent scholars of African art. These scholars are: Roy Sieber, Henry and Margaret Drewal, Paula Ben-Amos, Susan Vogel, Germaine Dieterlen, Marie-Louise Bastin, J. W. Mestach, Albert Maesen, Huguette Van Geluwe, Kate Ezra, Pascal James Imperato, Daniel Biebuyck, John Pemberton 3rd, Raoul Lehuard, Arthur Bourgeois, Kevin Carroll, Eberhard Fischer, Lorenz Homberger, Polly Nooter, Steven Tatum, François Neyt, Phillipe Guimiot, Bernard de Grunne, Piet Meyer, Barbara DeMott, Sidney Kasfir, Pierre Harter, and Malutshi Mudiji-Selenge. Marc Félix and his research assistants have provided invaluable data on the many objects Max and Betty purchased from him, reversing a long-standing tradition by which some dealers suppressed or ignored important details of origin and provenance.

I would like to thank the members of the board of the Stanley/University of Iowa Foundation Support Organization for encouragement and financial support for this and many other projects at The University of Iowa since 1978.

Finally, I would like to acknowledge the enormous encouragement and support, both moral and financial, that Max and Betty Stanley have provided since 1977, when I first visited Iowa looking for a job. They were willing to support me, although I had no experience and had not finished my degree, because they felt I showed promise. For six years they have funded the African art program in the School of Art and

Art History. They have allowed me to participate in the assembling of this fine collection, supported my applications for research leave and grants, and provided funds for Nora and our children to travel to Burkina Faso with me in 1984.

I wish Max were here now, but every time I pass the Chokwe chief figure I get the feeling that he is with us.

Christopher D. Roy, 1984

I would like to thank all of the people who have made the revised edition of *Art and Life in Africa* possible. The greatest change from the 1985 edition is the addition of objects that Betty collected from 1986 until her death in 1990. Kathy Neff has done an outstanding job of organizing production and overseeing the process at each step. Mark Tade, who produced the photographs for the 1985 volume, has made beautiful photographs of the objects collected here as well. Gail Zlatnik has edited the manuscripts and provided useful comments on the biography of Betty.

I am very grateful to the staff of The University of Iowa Museum of Art, especially Jo-Ann Conklin, David Dennis, Betty Breazeale, James Lindell, Jeff Martin, and the former curator of education Dr. Jane Ju, who have supported this effort in countless ways. I am grateful for the support and encouragement of the late Mary Kujawski-Roberts, Director of the University of Iowa Museum of Art.

My friend Marc Leo Félix visited Betty and me in Iowa and provided invaluable information on the provenance of objects he sold to Betty. I would also like to thank him here for the many important donations of African art he has made to The University of Iowa Museum of Art.

Finally, I would like to express my gratitude to Darrell Wyrick, president of The University of Iowa Foundation, and the directors of the Stanley/University of Iowa Foundation Support Organization. They have generously funded this and numerous other projects for the study of African art at The University of Iowa.

The contributors to this catalogue deserve special mention. Many graduate students have worked directly with objects in the collection over the past six years and have carried out research for seminars. The entries they have written are listed after their names. They include Emily Hanna-Vergara, Andrea Smith (nos. 24, 25, and 26), Kathryn Weinrich (nos. 4 and 28), Christina McOmber, Michael Matter (no. 32), Manuel Jordan (no. 21), Linda Green (no. 8), Victor Arango, Hashim Al-Tawil, Julie Risser, David A. Rowe, Dana L. Rush, Janet Hess, Ann Ciola, and Nicole Meyer.

I am especially grateful to my colleague Professor Allen F. Roberts of the departments of anthropology and African-American World Studies of The University of Iowa for contributing notes on objects he is particularly familiar with as a result of his research on the Tabwa and other peoples of eastern Zaire. These include entries no. 29, 30, 34, 35, and 36.

Christopher D. Roy, 1991

IN MEMORIAM

In the year of the Olympiad we met in Munich, and although we visited mainly museums and the opera, one day took us to the apartment of Ludwig Bretschneider, the pioneer German dealer of tribal art. It was here that Max and Betty Stanley each bought a "souvenir" to remind them of Munich. Max selected a Yoruba rider and Betty, a Cameroon clay pipe. Both were fine pieces and are still in the Stanley Collection.

A few years later, Max called to report: "Next to our motel room in Des Moines are some Africans with a good many artifacts. Why don't you give it a look, and if there is something interesting, I might buy it." I contacted the Africans but was not prepared for the arrival of several dealers in two vans. They brought a great deal of material, but little of quality except for utilitarian objects and a few masks. Max acquired a few.

Much has been written about the nature of collectors and what they have in common. I have discovered, however, that there are as many types of collectors as there are people and Max was no exception. Max the businessman set himself goals. One was to limit his purchase price to $2000 for one object. This guideline soon had to be broken when he discovered that quality, as he learned to recognize it, could not be acquired in such a manner. Cautions were thrown to the winds and a passionate collecting began by spending very respectable sums. Max became known as one of the most active collectors in America, and Muscatine, Iowa, became a magnet for the best American and European dealers. With experience, knowledge grew. The African art scholar Christopher Roy was appointed by the University. Professor Roy Sieber acted as a helpful consultant, and the dealers brought additional knowledge and their finest material. My role and Max's became reversed. It was now I who asked the questions and he who gave the answers. This became particularly evident when the collection branched out into unfamiliar areas.

Recently, I was grateful that after the crowded opening of the new Center for African Art in New York, I visited the Center a second time and met by chance Max and Betty. It was a day before his death. There were few people in the museum; Max, Betty, Marc Felix, Willy Mestach, Gaston de Havenon, and I. We reviewed leisurely the *Masterpieces from the Musee de l'Homme* and were spellbound by the simplest spoon figure from the Zulu (no. 99 in the catalogue) and compared it to Mestach's equally simple Tanzania figure in the Museum of Modern Art exhibition (no. 65 in the catalogue). We admired what we saw and searched to identify the sublime in African art. I believe we came close to it.

Ulfert Wilke
Director, The University of Iowa
Museum of Art, 1968–75

MAX STANLEY

1904–1984

TO MAX STANLEY

The many people at The University of Iowa and around the world who knew Max Stanley and who worked with him to build a fine collection of African sculpture feel a great sense of loss at his death. We will miss him grievously, but we will continue to derive enormous benefit from the study and enjoyment of the wonderful objects he collected and gave to the University and to the people of Iowa.

Betty Stanley began to collect African art in 1960 during a business trip the Stanleys made to West Africa. She flew to Ganta, Liberia, to visit Dr. and Mrs. George Harley. The Harleys were preparing to retire and were willing to sell some traditional objects they had collected over several decades. Betty purchased a few objects, including a gameboard that was displayed in the 1979 exhibition of the Stanley collection. In 1973, Ulfert Wilke, then Director of the University of Iowa Museum of Art, urged Max to begin collecting more seriously. The Stanleys visited a New York gallery where Max made his first purchase—an *ibeji* figure. The Stanleys were impressed by the quality and surprised by the prices of the objects they saw, and began to study, to subscribe to African art journals, and to visit increasing numbers of dealers in the United States and Europe. From 1973 to 1978 they purchased about 350 objects from all areas of Africa. They received helpful advice from Ulfert Wilke and from Roy Sieber, an alumnus of The University of Iowa, who was then teaching at Indiana University.

The Stanleys offered the collection to The University of Iowa, with the intention that it become the center for a program of African art studies. I came to the university in 1978 as the first professor of African art history. In 1979 the collection was exhibited at Iowa and a catalogue was published. A number of scholars of African art from three continents attended the opening and a conference at The School of Art and Art History. Max and Betty were so pleased by the praise their collection received from these visitors that, in the six years since 1979, they have redoubled their investment in the collection, both in terms of the time they devoted to collecting and the prices they were willing to pay for good sculpture. Max concentrated on seeking out high-quality objects, and with advice from me and from many other scholars, acquired many of the finest objects on the market. Objects that were considered to be of lesser quality were upgraded, and new types and styles were added. Max brought to collecting African art the same intensity and insistence on excellence that he devoted to his efforts for world peace through the Stanley Foundation, and to the many other projects with which he was involved. Since 1979 the collection has grown from 375 to 597 objects, of which 135 are selected for exhibition in *Art and Life in Africa*. (Of these, only fifteen were displayed in the 1979 exhibition.)

Max hoped that his collection of African art would stimulate interest in African art by students at Iowa, and he and Betty have supported the program since 1978 with funds for books, slides, faculty research, and student scholarships. Most of the collection has been on display in The University of Iowa Museum of Art since 1979, and many dozens of students have benefited from the opportunity to study these fine objects as subjects for research papers. I am grateful to Max and Betty for permitting me to help select new acquisitions. I have wonderful memories of evenings spent with them at their home looking at beautiful pieces, when Betty and I, and sometimes my wife Nora, would list our favorite pieces for Max, who always made the final choice. It has been a great privilege for me to work with Max for six years. I will miss him very much.

Christopher D. Roy
Curator of the Stanley Collection
Associate Professor of Art History,
The University of Iowa School
of Art and Art History

CATALOGUE OF THE
1985 EXHIBITION

Centers of Style of African Sculpture

In his 1935–38 four-volume study of African sculpture entitled *Centres de style de la sculpture negre africain*, Carl Kjersmeier first organized African art in a logical system that followed a geographical scheme and attempted to identify the tribal origins of the objects illustrated. He grouped together objects that were related geographically or culturally, and identified each style area with the colonial period name of the region.

In the half century since the publication of Kjersmeier's work, art historians have been successful in refining the techniques for attributing objects to ethnic groups on the basis of style. The greatest progress was made, especially in the 1960's, by William Fagg, former Keeper of African Collections in the Department of Ethnography of the British Museum. Mr. Fagg has published a number of landmark studies which have successfully identified the tribal origins of many very enigmatic objects, always with a sense of precision backed by a wealth of evidence that has inspired confidence in three generations of scholars, collectors, and museum curators. For some years scholars looked forward to each new publication that would attribute objects, previously thought familiar, to groups whose very names were widely unknown. Among these important contributions are *Nigerian Images* (1963), *African Sculpture* (1964 with Margaret Plass), *Tribes and Forms in African Art* (1965), *African Tribal Images: The Catherine White Reswick Collection* (1968), and *African Sculpture* (1970). Based on his own travels and research, and on study of public and private museums on three continents, Mr. Fagg was able to attribute objects to such little-known groups as the Badia, Mazinga, Gwandara, Alangua, BaSolongo, WaZiba, Mambunda, BaKwese, Kana, Basa Komo, Ishan, Ngombe, Ngumba, BaDondo, Bena Biombo, WaDumbo, WaKerewe, and Anguru—to name just a few. Mr. Fagg began what students of African art have been doing ever since, which is to compare all the objects attributed to a given group on acquisition cards in museums all over the world and then to define accurately and thus successfully the characteristics of each group's style. It is not surprising that in some cases the corpus of a group's artistic production consists of one or two objects in old collections in German, French, Portuguese or British ethnography museums. To Mr. Fagg's credit, he noted that it is not always possible to trace clear distinctions between the styles of one tribe and the next, and that one must use "a broken line where the artistic frontier is 'open', permitting stylistic influences to pass in one direction or both . . ." (1965:13).

An entirely new approach was first elaborated in print in *Open Frontiers: The Mobility of Art in Black Africa* by René Bravmann for the Henry Art Gallery, University of Washington (1973). Professor Bravmann suggested that the "tribality" of African art, in which the distribution of a group's particular style is necessarily limited to the area populated by the tribe, may be a "dreadful oversimplification . . . a decided falsification of the very life of art in Black Africa." He added that, "the movement of shrines, spirit forces, and individual religious specialists and believers has made the area of art and religion an extremely fluid one. These avenues of mobility and change destroy the 'walls' that have been built about African cultures and their arts and point to the very open frontiers, both geographic and conceptual, that exist between them" (1973:9–10). Bravmann described the movement of art from one group to another through trade, and he noted the presence of workshops of artists who sell their work over a large area as an important factor in the diffusion of objects and styles.

I would like to advance this idea of open frontiers between ethnic groups an additional step by suggesting that there are important centers of style throughout Africa where families, clans, and workshops produce sculpture and other art that is dispersed over a large, pan-tribal, geographical style area. A family of artists belonging to a single ethnic group may produce sculpture on commission for several neighboring tribes. Such family workshops may even adjust the "tribal style" in which they carve, to produce objects in the local style of their clients, contributing to a marked homogeneity of styles in an area and much confusion on the part of art historians who attempt to assign particular objects to individual groups on the basis of style. Such "Centers of Style" have been described in the past, notably the "Ogowe River Style" of Gabon, where the Punu, Lumbu, Ashira, and others use masks representing the spirits of deceased maidens in a very uniform style. Here, it appears, masks are carved by the Punu and traded to many other groups who use them in similar performances. Similarly, in the grasslands of Cameroon, a workshop in one small kingdom—Kom, for example—may provide

---

Left: **Two Nuna masks in the village of Serena, March 5, 1984.**
Both masks were carved by Karim Konaté, from Ouri. The masks appeared for the burial of an elder earth-priest of the Tiateba family in Serena. Foreground *zonie*, "speak a word" (speak up to protect your children from witchcraft); background *durbisie*, "run without resting" (be careful of sorcery).

Carvers of the Konaté family in Ouri, April 20, 1984.

Left to right: Bomavay, Hezuma, Poboye, apprentice, Yekiné, apprentice, Karim.

masks and other carvings to neighboring kingdoms, resulting in a homogeneous style best described as the "Cameroon Grasslands Style." Other centers of style exist among the Luba of southeastern Zaire, who produce sculpture for the Songye and other neighboring groups, among the Ibo of southeastern Nigeria, among the Akan of Ghana and Ivory Coast (as described by René Bravmann), and in many other areas.

The "Center of Style" with which I am most familiar, and to which I will devote the rest of this essay, is located in the village of Ouri, in central Burkina Faso (Upper Volta). Ouri is a village of mixed Ko, Dyula, Bwa, and Nuna population, on the road that leads north from Boromo to Safané, just west of the Black Volta River. Ouri was first occupied by the Ko and Nuna, groups that have been referred to in the past by the Moré (Mossi) pejorative, "gurunsi." Sometime in the early nineteenth century, several Dyula families, of which the most important is still the Fofana family, settled in Ouri, creating an important center for trade in kola nuts and gold from Ghana, and in slaves captured among the small farmer groups in southern Burkina Faso. Not long after the Dyula merchants arrived in Ouri, the senior male elder of the Fofana family invited families of the Konaté blacksmith clan to settle in a neighborhood on the western side of the village and to provide hoes and other iron tools for the farmers in the village. The Konaté are a blacksmith clan of Mandé origin. Led by the "founding ancestors," Woronfé and Leileko Konaté, they had migrated from the Mandé area of what is now Mali, by way of the Bobo village of Kapo, near Bobo-Dioulasso, to the Bwa and Marka Dafing town of Ouakara (Wakara), about sixty-five kilometers west of Ouri. There they had settled and produced forged tools for the Bwa and Marka farmers in the area, adopting Bwamu (the language of the Bwa) as their clan language. To this day the Konaté speak Bwamu among themselves, although they also speak the language of their Ko, Nuna, Marka, and Dyula clients. The migration from Ouakara to Ouri was led by Kakamo, six generations ago.

Earlier generations of Konaté, in Ouakara and Ouri, had carved objects of wood, including masks, but the craft was abandoned for many years until the time of Nani, grand-uncle of the current generation of artists. Nani was the younger brother of Lihani, whose eldest son was Niposi, father of Mibieni, Poboye, Nazin, Naziko, Tiesie, and Tihia, some of whom now carve in Ouri. In the early 1960's Nani died childless, but he passed on his artistic genius to his brother's sons. Lihani's younger son was Dubata, who still lives in Ouri, and who was a great carver and passed his skill to his son, Karim. Dubata is also a diviner of great reputation among the blacksmiths and farmers of Ouri and surrounding villages.

Currently the most active Konaté sculptors in Ouri are Poboye, Naziko, Bomavay, Tangin, Hezuma, Yekiné, and Karim, assisted by many younger brothers and nephews (page 4). During the dry season from February to May, 1984, when I lived in Ouri, these carvers received commissions from mask-owning clans in the Nuna villages of Serena (page 2), Tissé, Lasso, and Tierkou; the Marka Dafing villages of Bona, Oumina, and Koamba; the Ko villages of Oulo, Ouarabuno; the Bwa villages of Bagassi, Houndé, Pa, and Boni; and from Ouri itself (page 6). In addition they carved masks in the Bwa style for their own use. An elder brother, Mahama Konaté, left Ouri about seven years ago and moved with his family to Nouna, in northwestern Burkina Faso, only 180 km.

from the border with Mali. There he carves masks and other wooden objects for the northern Bwa and the Bobo-Fing in Tansilla, Solenzo, and in several other villages near Nouna.

I attended several mask performances—funerals, initiations, and village purification ceremonies—at which masks carved by living and deceased sculptors of the Konaté family participated. The most spectacular, in terms of size, quality of carving, and performance, were three Nuna masks in Serena carved by Karim (page 2). Other Nuna masks at Tissé and Tierko, and Ko masks in Ouri, were indistinguishable from older masks (at the same performances or in collections outside of Africa) which had been carved by the now deceased elder Konaté.

Not only does the Konaté family in Ouri produce objects for five major neighboring ethnic groups, they also produce large numbers of masks for the tourist trade in Ouagadougou. They refer to these as "copies," and are able to distinguish clearly between traditional masks for use by local villagers, and tourist "copies" to be sold in Ouagadougou. They distinguish between them on the basis of style, quality, and whether or not the necessary sacrifices were done during the carving process—sacrifices which make a traditional mask function effectively. Members of the family make frequent trips to Ouagadougou by motor-bike, so laden with tourist masks that only the rider's head rises above the load of carvings strung around him. (They had spent three months producing the twelve masks I saw on one load headed for Ouaga.) The favorite models, sold in largest numbers, are the "butterfly" masks based on Bwa and Nuna prototypes, and the round "sun" masks (masque soleil) popular since one appeared on the cover of Henri Kamer's catalogue of Voltaic sculpture (page 8). The active carvers in the family state that they began to produce copies for tourists soon after Upper Volta's independence in 1960. At that time, the farmers in the Ouri region increasingly became part of a cash economy, and ceased exchanging crops for the tools, weapons, and masks produced by the Konaté. The traditional relationship between the blacksmiths and farmers of Ouri broke down. Earlier, when a farmer needed an iron hoe blade, it was produced by a smith, who was then free to take payment in grain from the farmer's granary at any time during the year. At about the time of independence, farmers began to purchase hoes from itinerant smiths in the Ouri market. The Konaté could no longer survive simply by making hoes and masks, and so were forced to carve copies to sell in Ouagadougou, Abidjan, and Bobo-Dioulasso. In about 1977, on one of the frequent trips he made to sell masks in Ouagadougou, Poboye Konaté visited a Mossi dealer who accompanied him to the old I. F. A. N. art museum, whose director was then Toumani Triandé. (This is now part of the national scientific research center, C. N. R. S. T.) The dealer, Issa Ouedraogo, pointed out several of the museum's masks, especially Mossi plank masks. The dealer wanted copies, and so, during the next several weeks, Poboye produced them.

With the exception of the Bobo-Fing masks carved by Mahama in Nouna, and occasionally those done by sculptors in Ouri for the tourist trade, the work of the Konaté family workshop all belongs to the "Central Voltaic Style Area." This area includes the styles of the Nuna, Ko, Lela, southwestern Mossi, Bwa, and Marka Dafing, each of which is characterized by the red, white, and black geometric patterns that elaborate the masks' surfaces and especially by the distinctive concentric

circles of the "Upper Volta target motif." Vertical planks or blades appear on all but southwestern Mossi and Lela masks, and all are two-dimensional face masks, rather than the helmet mask type favored by the Bobo-Fing. In most of the villages in the valley of the Black Volta River between the Ghana border and the city of Nouna, mask carving is dominated by the Konaté carvers in Ouri, either because several of the village masks have been carved in Ouri, or because local carvers have seen Konaté masks used in nearby villages and have imitated them. Carvers in Houndé and Boni have acknowledged to me the importance of the influence of the Konaté style on their own work. They are aware that the Konaté receive many commissions, and that imitations of their work attract clients.

The active Konaté sculptors are able to distinguish the characteristics of the five styles in which they carve, and will point to the foliate patterns that radiate from the eyes of a Nuna mask, or the diamond-shaped mouth of many Ko masks, as characteristics of a particular tribal style that must be included to satisfy their clients. Nevertheless, their work is very homogeneous in terms of proportions, composition, color, and technique. In addition, the tribal styles of this area are so homogeneous that few casual spectators can tell them apart. In the past six years, numerous scholars of African art, involved with public or private collections that include masks from the area, have called me to seek help identifying the styles of groups in this area. Although the Konaté can identify the styles they carve, the characteristic patterns are so subtly different that few people outside of the area can distinguish Nuna masks from Ko or Bwa masks. The importance of the Konaté workshop style complements the importance of Nuna masks in central Burkina Faso. The similarity between the Nuna, Ko, and Bwa styles is the result of the work of the Konaté, and of the fact that the Bwa have "borrowed" their wooden mask-carving tradition from the Ko and Nuna. Until the mid-nineteenth century, the Bwa (often called Bobo-Oulé in earlier literature) did not use wooden masks. The many broad, tall plank masks decorated with black and white checkerboard patterns that have been illustrated so often in studies of African art were obtained by the southern Bwa in the villages of Boni, Dossi, and more recently Pa, from the Nuna and Ko, who have traditionally used them. The earliest use of plank masks by the Bwa dates from a raid by warriors from the Bwa village of Boni on a Nuna village. The Bwa stole all the Nuna masks and carried them off to Boni. This raid took place before the arrival of the French in 1897 and yet it is still customary for the head of the Bondé family in Boni to purchase new masks from the Konaté workshop in Ouri, rather than to commission them from Bwa carvers in the closer village of Houndé. Although detailed studies have yet to be carried out, it seems very possible that the Nuna have influenced not only the Bwa, but also the Marka Dafing, the Lela, and by extension the southwestern Mossi, all of whom belong to the central Voltaic style area.

It is not unusual for a family or workshop to produce masks for a number of communities spread over a broad area belonging to a single ethnic group. This has occurred frequently in Africa, and elsewhere in the world. During the Classic period in pre-Columbian Mexico, the potters of Teotihuacan produced pieces made of a "thin orange" clay body, in the Teotihuacan style, that was dispersed by trade all over Mexico. Art historians can cite additional examples from Europe, China, India, and North America. It is far more unusual, however, to find a single workshop producing sculpture for five different ethnic groups, in styles which, although identifiable by the carvers and owners, are so homogeneous that no one else can tell them apart. When, in the past, the work of a single hand or workshop has been discovered, either being used by living groups or in an archaeological context in widely scattered sites, it has been assumed that the diffusion of art was the result of long-distance trade. Perhaps historians of African art should now ask if objects in similar or identical styles were produced in "Centers of Style," where artists belonging to one ethnic group produced art for all of their neighbors. Perhaps it is even more important to cease attempting to break down large regional styles into finer and finer tribal styles and substyles, and to recognize that artists in Africa are capable of producing work not only in their own style, but in the styles of their neighbors. It is clear that, at least in central Burkina Faso, we cannot tell which group produced an object by analyzing fine style characteristics.

In the catalogue "Art and Life in Africa: Selections from the Stanley Collection," there are several objects that have been assigned to little-known ethnic groups such as the Lula, Maravi, and Malungu on the basis of minor style variations that barely distinguish them from the work of their neighbors. Perhaps here the larger style area designations, such as "Kwango/Kwilu Rivers Basin" or "Sankuru/Lualaba Rivers/ Lake Tanganyika Area," are more valid and useful means for classifying these objects than finer tribal designations would be. I myself may have erred in attempting to define too carefully the characteristics of these styles, when these may be the work of "Centers of Style of African Sculpture."

Left: **Ko mask carved by a sculptor of the Konaté family for the Naniabô neighborhood in Ouri.**
Mask is named *kanabadidie* "a woman does not own a house" (you cannot take anything out of this world). For a performance on March 10, 1984 to clear the neighborhood of evil spirits.

Bomavay Konaté carving a sun mask for sale to tourists in Ouagadougou, April, 1984.

WESTERN SUDAN

JENNE
DOGON
BAMANA
Niger River
BAGA
MOSSI
BWA
NUNA
LOBI
Volta R.
SENUFO
Bandama R.
Benue R.
Cross River

The Western Sudan Style Area

"Sudan," from the Arabic *bilad es sudan*, "Land of the Blacks," is the name of a broad climatic zone that stretches across Africa from the Atlantic Ocean to the Red Sea, from the Sahara in the north to the forest regions of the Guinea Coast in the south. The area is characterized near the desert by open, grassy parklands with widely scattered trees and in the south by denser woodlands. In recent years the area has suffered long periods of drought, causing widespread starvation of humans and livestock as well as overgrazing which further contributes to the rapid southward movement of desert sands into what were once arable regions. The most important geographical features are the Niger River, which rises in the highlands of Guinea and curves north and then southeast into Nigeria, and the Red, White, and Black branches of the Volta River, all of which flow to the sea through Ghana.

A short rainy reason from June to September (longer in the south) permits subsistence farming. The staple crops have been pearl millet, sorghum, sesame, and cotton, and after their arrival from the New World, corn and peanuts. Sorghum especially is brewed into mildly alcoholic beer, a staple of social and ritual activity. During the long dry season from October to May, when farming is impossible, people engage in part-time craft specialties including the forging of iron tools, the forming and firing of pottery, weaving, basket-making, carving, and in the performing of masks associated with funerals, initiations, and village purification ceremonies.

Long before the arrival of the first Europeans in the mid-nineteenth century, the peoples of the Sudan had created great political states, including Ghana (eighth–eleventh centuries), Mali (thirteenth–sixteenth centuries), Songhai (fifteenth–sixteenth centuries) and Mossi (fifteenth–nineteenth centuries). In several of these states the written records kept by Arabic chroniclers have been preserved, so we know, for example, that Timbuktu was an important center of trade and learning until it was sacked by the Mossi in the mid-thirteenth century.

The influence of Islam has waxed and waned in the area, spread primarily along trade routes by Moslem merchants, but also by holy wars in the nineteenth century. With some exceptions the spread of Islam has had an adverse effect on the production and use of traditional sculpture; visitors to the area are finding more and more villages where sculpture has disappeared with the conversion of the populace to Islam.

The sculptural style of the Western Sudan, west of the Niger River, is dominated by the work of two major groups: (1) the Mandé-speakers who live primarily in western Upper Volta, Mali, and northern Ivory Coast in the valley of the upper Niger River, and (2) the Gur-speaking peoples of Upper Volta (recently renamed Burkina Faso), of northern Ghana and Togo, in the basin of the upper Volta Rivers. The Upper Niger River Style is characterized by the use of a "T"-shaped meeting of the nose and brow, with the eyes often high in the intersection on flat, broad cheeks. Colors are generally dark, either black or natural-wood brown, although many groups produce colorful cloth masquerades, and the Bobo paint their masks red, white, and blue. Figures are tall and attenuated, with cylindrical torsos flanked by arms that are held at the sides, upper arms parallel to the torso and forearms at a sharp angle almost parallel to the ground. Scarification patterns are burned into the wood with a heated blade, and the entire surface of the carving may be seared black. In contrast, the sculptors of the Upper Volta River Style area break up the surfaces of masks and figures with dramatic combinations of red, white, and black geometric patterns, especially a distinctive system of concentric circles around the eyes—the "Upper Volta target motif." Masks are freshly painted before each performance, so that even ancient masks show brilliant new colors. The Mossi, Bwa, Ko, and Nuna in Burkina Faso carve masks with tall, two-dimensional planks rising above the face. Throughout the Western Sudan, groups produce horizontal masks that combine the powerful features of several animals. In both style areas women have worn their hair in a distinctive sagittal crest, a feature frequently represented on their carved figures.

Among Mandé-speakers, masks are used primarily for the initiations of men into successively higher initiatory grades, although they also appear for the funerals of society members. Among Gur-speakers, masks are owned by families and clans, and appear at the funerals of elder men and women of the family. They also may play a role in the initiation of men and women into the secrets of masks' performances, and they act the parts of characters in stories of the history of the clan. Figures are used in both areas for a multitude of purposes, including the encouragement of human, animal, and agricultural fertility, the commemoration of ancestors, and the contacting of the protective spirits who watch over the family or community.

It is interesting to note that although sculptural traditions described in the nineteenth century have disappeared in areas of Africa where groups are receptive to European and Moslem changes, nevertheless in many parts of the Sudan groups have resisted acculturation vigorously, and so it is still possible to visit communities where ritual life goes on today very much as it did a hundred years ago.

1. JENNE CULTURE, Mali / Figure couple / Fired clay / H. 18 cm., L. Base 19 cm. (H. 7″, L. Base 7½″)

In March 1943, the French archaeologist Theodore Monod discovered a fired clay figure of a kneeling woman at a site called Kaniana, 2 kilometers from the modern city of Djenne, in Mali (Leiris and Delange 1968: frontispiece). Since that time a large number of objects in clay, iron, bronze, and gold have been excavated—primarily from the *tumuli*, high mounds of earth that rise above the floodwaters of the Niger. These objects were created by a culture that flourished there, in the area of the Inland Delta of the Niger River, from about 750 to 1650 A.D. Very few of these objects have been discovered by trained archaeologists, however. Many more have been dug up by local treasure hunters working at Jenne burial sites.

These objects include a broad range of iconographic types, including large figures of warriors mounted on horses (or donkeys), kneeling male and female figures, humans covered with what appear to be disease pustules, groups of figures surrounding a larger female, and especially, humans covered with snakes. Indeed, the serpent motif is by far the most common pattern in the Jenne style, and must indicate the importance of snakes in the religious belief of the Jenne culture.

While much Jenne sculpture bears beautiful details of dress, weaponry, and body paint or scarification, few portray the degree of emotion expressed by this figure pair. They embrace with great sorrow, cheek-to-cheek, with their arms over each other's shoulders. One can only imagine that they depict two wives mourning the passing of their husband, as he perhaps lies buried nearby in a funerary urn.

The couple has been dated by the Oxford University laboratories through the use of thermoluminescence to 625 years ago (+/− 95 years).

2. JENNE CULTURE, Mali / Mask / Fired clay / W. 17 cm. (7")

In the past few years a number of exhibitions and catalogues have been devoted to the art of the Jenne culture. Typically, they have shown large numbers of fired clay figurines and figures of serpents, occasionally the large, finely decorated jars with which these objects are found, and very rarely, some of the small bronzes, beads and other artifacts of the Jenne people, who lived in the region for almost two thousand years—beginning in the third century B.C. and continuing into the seventeenth century A.D. when they abandoned that site.

Only two other masks, both in bronze, have been published (de Grunne 1980b: 117,119). Both of them lack eye openings, and are much too small to have been worn over the face. In contrast, the present example is large and does provide for the wearer's sight. (We do not know, however, if the mask was intended for the living or the dead.) A bit of stylized beard rims the right cheek. Heavily incised patterns of diagonal lines cover the face, and a serpent extends down the forehead and nose. These marks may have represented painted patterns or scars.

3. JENNE CULTURE, Mali / Mother and child / Fired clay / H. 29 cm. (11″)

"Maternity" figures are fairly common in Jenne sculpture. Yet in some cases the "child" is a full-grown adult with weapons, beard, and helmet. Here, as elsewhere more recently in Africa, the reference is to a generalized, primordial ancestress, rather than to an individual mother. The figure, and especially the stylization of the child, should be compared to the Senufo "maternity" (no. 11).

The figure wears a necklace in the shape of a serpent, an important motif in Jenne sculpture.

The Oxford University laboratories have used the thermoluminescence technique to date the object to 700 years ago (+/− 150 years).

4. JENNE CULTURE, Mali / Mounted warrior / Bronze / H. 9.2 cm. (4")

Among the best known and most eagerly sought objects produced by the Jenne culture are the large, fired clay figures of mounted warriors (de Grunne 1980b: 76–83). These are notable for the attention given to details such as the saddle, bridle, and the weapons and clothing of the warrior. In this example, a master bronze caster has carefully scaled down all this exquisite detail to produce a miniature of great delicacy and beauty. Even the braided pattern of the reins, the horse's mane, the tiny quiver of arrows, and the scarification patterns on the head and face can be seen through the thin, light green patina. The figure also clearly bears the elongated head, bulging eyes, and everted lips that are characteristic of the sculptural style of the Jenne culture.

There is no evidence of how the object was used: no loops or rings to suggest the figure was worn as a pendant, no signs of wear to provide a clue as to how it was handled.

5. JENNE CULTURE, Mali / Figure covered with snakes / Fired clay / H. 23.5 cm. (9″)

This figure is literally covered with snakes. Bernard de Grunne has written that: "The frequency of the motif may be explained by the importance of the serpent in the cosmology of the Soninke and the mythical origins of the Wagadou empire. It records the story of a python called Wagadou Bida, born of the first marriage of Dinga, the head of a Soninke clan and father of the founder of the Wagadou empire. Wagadou Bida is presented in this myth as the first occupant of the land and also the guarantee of the empire's continuing existence. The annual sacrifice of a virgin was necessary to ensure its continuity. One day, a Soninke crazed with grief at the thought that the young girl he loved would be sacrificed that year, killed the serpent. A devastating drought followed his act and the ruin of the empire ensued. The resulting famine caused the Soninke to disperse. One of Djenne's foundations is said to date from this period" (de Grunne 1981 : 11).

The figure has been dated by thermoluminescence to 600 years ago (+/− 70 years).

6. JENNE CULTURE, Mali / Kneeling Woman / Fired clay / H. 23 cm. (9")

This kneeling female figure bears incised patterns that represent bracelets on her wrists and a double strand of beads at her neck. She kneels, looking slightly upward, in a pose that is among the most common in Jenne statuary.

In an earlier catalogue of African art in Iowa collections, I noted the similarities between certain gestures that appear frequently in Jenne sculpture and gestures that are used to this day among groups living in the bend of the Niger River

(Roy 1981 : 39). Here, for example, this female figure kneels in a pose of humility and respect, the same pose women throughout Burkina Faso assume when they serve a meal or a bowl of millet beer to their male relatives. It seems that, lacking more substantial evidence of the people who made these objects, we can interpret many of their cultural patterns by comparing their artifacts with the material cultures of living peoples.

7. BAMANA (Bambara), Mali / Female figure / Wood, textile / H. 60.3 cm. (23″)

Recent research by Kate Ezra has added significantly to our understanding of the function of certain types of Bamana figures: "This sculpture resembles the figures, called *nyeleni*, that are associated with new male initiates of the *Jo* society. Following their initiation the young men travel to surrounding villages where they present performances that simultaneously show off their new status as initiates and provide entertainment. The initiates are divided into groups with distinctive costumes, songs, music, dances, and sculpture. The groups of initiates who are from blacksmith families are most often said to incorporate figure sculptures into their performances. The sculptures are placed on the dance area (hence the base on this figure) and are also held while dancing. These sculptures are usually lavishly ornamented with beads, metal rings, loincloths, and head ties, and have incised scarification marks covering the torso, chest, arms, backs of the legs, and face. The figures are jokingly referred to as the 'girlfriends' of the young men, and the cloth and jewelry increase their attractiveness" (Ezra 1984).

The style of this figure, with its sagittal crest and its heart-shaped face and protruding mouth, bears a strong resemblance to the northern Senufo sculpture style. This indicates that the figure was carved by a Bamana artist in southern Mali where Senufo cultural influences are particularly strong. Kate Ezra notes that the area in which the *Jo* society is found extends to the border of Ivory Coast where contact with the Senufo is likely.

8. BAMANA (Bambara), Mali / Female figure / Wood / H. 46.3 cm. (18″)

This spectacular Bamana figure of a woman stands proudly erect—great, flipper-like hands held palms forward. Large, conical breasts jut from the shoulders. The torso is long and cylindrical, with a slightly swollen abdomen. The feet are large to provide a firm support. Complex patterns of chip-carved scarification marks circle the breasts, cross the chest, and band the shoulders and arms. The most distinctive feature is the head, with its long, pointed nose, eyes perched high in the intersection of nose and brow, and the elegant cascading hairstyle that spans the head from side to side.

This is one of a large number of figures and masks that share identical stylistic features. Allen Wardwell first described this style (Wardwell 1966), which must be the achievement of a large workshop in southeastern Mali. There are seated figures in the collections of the University Museum, University of Pennsylvania (acquired in 1927), the British Museum (ac-

quired in 1919), and the Henri Kamer collection. The seated figure formerly in the collection of Pierre Matisse and published in 1917, is said to have come from Bobo-Dioulasso (then the colonial capital of this part of French West Africa). There are standing figures in the Sainsbury collection in London, the Rockefeller collection at the Metropolitan Museum of Art, and the National Museum of African Art in Washington. The most spectacular, a horse and rider at the Musée de l'Homme, was acquired in 1933. The acquisition card indicates that it came from "Segou Secoro" one of the neighborhoods of Segou, which leads us to the very tentative assumption that all were produced in Segou (Wardwell 1966: 112–3). The slight variations in details and proportions, however, indicate that these are the work of many hands, rather than the oeuvre of a single artist (Bassani 1978; Kate Ezra 1984).

9. BAMANA, Mali / Dance crest, *chi wara* / Wood / H. 58.7 cm. (23")

This delicate dance crest was carved in the eastern Bamana area near the city of Segou on the Niger River. It represents the female oryx antelope (*Oryx beisa*) carrying her young on her back the way human mothers carry their children.

Such objects are worn in male/female pairs by Bamana men who are members of the *chi wara* association, the second most important of the six Bamana men's societies. The function of the *chi wara* is to teach the skills needed for successful farming, to ensure a good harvest, and to guarantee the survival of the Bamana. The crests are worn in dances accompanied by women singing songs in praise of the ideal farmer. The dancer imitates the bounding leaps of the antelope and emits sharp cries as the best young farmers in the community

wildly hoe the ground around them. The pairing of the antelope crests represents the essential union between men and women to produce new generations, and between sun and earth to produce new crops.

This crest is unusually small and delicate. It is remarkable for the duplicate curves of the necks and the upward thrust of the horns of the female and her male young. The crest is uniformly covered with a thick layer of soot from the fires in the kitchen where it was stored. Repeated handling has polished the figures' necks to a high gloss. Burned-in scars and other decorative patterns are just visible on each antelope's forehead and face.

10. SENUFO, Ivory Coast / Face mask, *kpeli-yëhë* or *kodöli-yëhë* / Wood / H. 34.9 cm. (14″)

With its broad, flat, curving horns, its bulging forehead, and its long, bovine snout, this face mask looks very much like a buffalo. In Poro symbolism the buffalo, *noo*, is very important. ". . . A primary meaning of the buffalo motif is the celebration of advancement and regeneration in the *poro* cycle, the path to adulthood and fulfillment." *Poro* initiates are considered children of the "Ancient Mother," but only a slight tonal change distinguishes the *poro* words for "mother" and "buffalo." "In view of this density of meaning, it is hardly sur-

prising that buffalo horns figure so prominently in the face mask iconography of many different Senufo groups" (Glaze in Vogel 1981 : 41–2).

This *kpeli-yëhë* is remarkable for the severe simplicity of its forms, contrasting strongly with the cluttered, busy surfaces of most Senufo face masks. It is also illustrated in the catalogue of the de Havenon collection (de Havenon 1971 : no. 100).

11. SENUFO, Ivory Coast and Burkina Faso / Mother and Child / Wood / H. 49.2 cm. (19⅜")

At the simplest, most exoteric level, this figure represents maternity—the mother suckling her child. But here, as in most African art, there is a more profound, esoteric meaning. Describing a somewhat larger but otherwise very similar figure in the Tishman collection, Gilbert Bochet has written: "The figure represents the old mother of the village (*kaa tyeleo*), the central divinity of the initiation cycle (*poro*). She absorbs adolescents not yet seen as human—the nearly shapeless infant. (In this function, she is symbolized by the panther.) After having nursed them, as shown here, with the milk of knowledge, she redelivers them as initiates, complete human beings" (Bochet in Vogel 1981:46). The figure also reminds the Senufo that the first *poro* society belonged to women,

who held all power in the community until the creator god, *Kolotyoloo*, seized *poro* and gave it to men to punish women for their wickedness. Such figures are placed in the *sinzanga*, sacred forest grove of the men's society. There, the men are responsible for making blood sacrifices to the children of the Ancient Mother—the ancestors—so that they will intercede for the benefit of the community of the living (Glaze 1981:92–3).

In Western art we are used to relaxed and warm maternity figures. In contrast, this mother figure is tense and iconic as she stares fixedly into space, her back arched and arms rigid, barely touching the embryonic figure of the "child" to the tip of her breast.

12. SENUFO, Ivory Coast and Burkina Faso / Helmet mask, *kponyungo* / Wood / L. 104 cm. (41″)

Senufo helmet masks—elaborate assemblages of antelope horns, bush-pig tusks, rows of enormous sharp teeth, and the figures of birds and chameleons—are called *kponyungo* or "funeral head mask." Helmet masks serve in the senior and most dangerous of the masquerades used by the Senufo *poro* society. "They are the embodiment of supernatural powers and knowledge of magical formulae, expressed through aggressive forms and symbols . . . These powers are augmented by age and validated by the accretion of magical substances and blood sacrifices to . . . the ancestors and the bush spirits. The masquerade incarnates powers that may be directed against lawbreakers and sorcerers and against negative spirit forces, such as witches, wandering dead, and malevolent bush spirits" (Glaze 1981 : 207–8).

The mask performer plays a double-membrane barrel drum and wears a costume that consists of a one-piece suit dyed deep red and painted with figurative and geometric patterns. Because the costume is not attached to the mask, holes are not pierced around the base or neck of the mask. The performer is able to see out through the open jaws.

This large, elegant example is particularly notable for the stylization of the chameleon and hornbill (bird) forms. I find especially beautiful the way the spherical eye is set on the smooth curved line joining the nose and cheek.

13. SENUFO, Ivory Coast / Mask, *kpeli-yëhë* or *kodöli-yëhë* / Wood / H. 27.9 cm. (11")

Masks of this type have been called *keplié* in the past, a French version of the Senufo *kpeli-yëhë* (Kafiri dialect) or *kodöli-yëhë* (Kufuru dialect), which mean "face mask."

Face masks represent the female element, helmet masks the male in funeral performances involving Senufo blacksmiths. "The abstract forms of the mask are not meant to be a naturalistic portrait; rather, the finely drawn contours and textures of the face mask, as well as the artistry of the dancer, are intended to be beautiful as a young woman is beautiful. Sometimes called 'girlfriend' or 'wife' of a male-associated masquerade or spirit . . . the face masquerade is always intended to 'be beautiful' in praise of a man or youth on the oc-

casion of his commemorative funeral" (Glaze 1981 : 127–32).

Wooden Senufo face masks usually include a crest in the center of the forehead, flanked by a vertical pair of horns. Here, however, there are no horns, and the crest has taken the shape of a stylized bird's beak and projects gracefully forward and down across the face. The intended meaning of such a crest can only be interpreted by the original owner, but the vertical line that frames the face, we know represents a traditional women's hairstyle. The tiny, protuberant mouth, the long, thin nose, and the heart-shaped outline of the brows and cheeks are common characteristics of the *kpeli-yëhë* masquerade.

14. DOGON, Mali and Burkina Faso / Figure of a musician / Wood / H. 66 cm. (26")

This large figure of a musician bears many of the most characteristic traits of the Dogon figure style. The nose is shaped like the head of an arrow, the ears are C-shaped, and the figure wears a jutting, spade-shaped beard. The chest muscles, so heavy they resemble female breasts, form a yoke that reflects the angle of the solid thighs. The upper arms are suspended from this pectoral yoke so that they hang parallel to the torso. The figure's surface is severely worn, and is sticky from successive and generous applications of cosmetic vegetable fat from the shea-nut tree (*Butyrospermum parkii*).

The figure is playing a balafon—a musical instrument composed of wooden bars of graduated lengths; beneath which large dried-gourd resonators are suspended. The bars are struck with wooden hammers (missing from this figure). The balafon can be placed on the ground or can be carried suspended by a cotton band that passes around the neck, as here. Throughout Mali, Burkina Faso, and northern Ivory Coast, balafon music accompanies mask performances. Jean Laude described only two figures of musicians in his catalogue of the Lester Wunderman collection (Laude 1973:51). A figure playing a lute was once in the Kamer collection, and a pair of seated figures playing a balafon is in the Rockefeller collection at the Metropolitan Museum of Art (Newton 1978:151).

15. DOGON, Mali and Burkina Faso / Ancestor couple / Wood / H. 75 cm. (30")

Large male-female couples like this one were placed in Dogon village shrines where they represented the mythical progenitors of the Dogon, the primordial couple born before the four other *nommo* pairs at the creation. Such figures received sacrifices intended to protect the entire community from disaster of any kind.

The rigid, frontal formality of the composition contrasts rather strikingly with the implication of tenderness and affection in the male's embrace of the female. Barbara DeMott writes: "To the Dogon a male-female pair represents a positive statement of sexual unity, order, and harmony. The male figure has his arm around the female figure. This gesture visually links the couple and creates a dramatic horizontal line which balances the vertical thrust of the forms of the sculpture. These interlocking verticals and horizontals compose the pair and create a checkerboard conceived three-dimensionally as the interpenetration of solid and void. In Dogon art and myth, the checkerboard is a symbol for ordered human culture. Numerology underscores the meaning of the checkerboard. Three, the male number, and four, the female number, can be clearly read in the arrangement of their limbs and torso. The number two, which is implied by the couple, refers to the ideal of pairing essential for fertility and productivity in Dogon thought" (DeMott:1984).

The theme of the ancestral pair occurs frequently in Africa, especially among the Dogon. Other well known Dogon examples include the couple from the Wunderman collection in the Metropolitan Museum of Art, and the large pair in the Museum Rietberg Zurich. Since 1979 I have examined the latter on three occasions and I am convinced that they came from the same workshop, and perhaps are by the same hand (cf. Leuzinger 1960:83).

16., 17. DOGON (Tellem style), Mali and Burkina Faso / Pair of female figures / Wood / H. (undamaged figure) 50.5 cm. (20")

Dogon oral history indicates that they migrated into the area they now inhabit from the northwest. At the end of their migration they encountered a group called Tellem, associated by some scholars with the modern Kurumba who now live in northern Burkina Faso (Upper Volta). Objects found in burials high above villages now inhabited by the Dogon have been attributed to the earlier Tellem population, although there is considerable disagreement among scholars about the true character of the Tellem/Dogon relationship.

Germaine Dieterlen has attributed these ancient figures to the Tellem on the basis of style: "the hands placed on the thighs, rather than on the abdomen, prominent and natural-istic breasts, plaited hairstyle, and especially the abdominal scarification . . . indicate that these statuettes are probably Tellem" (Dieterlen 1984).

These figures were found together, associated with a burial in one of the numerous small cliffs high in the Bandiagara escarpment. In the bone-dry caves of the region, almost free of the insects and bacteria that might have caused them to decay, such objects have survived for centuries. Wooden objects from other burials in these cliffs have been radiocarbon-dated to as early as 1200 A.D..

18. DOGON, Mali and Burkina Faso / Mask, *Satimbe* / Wood / H. 127 cm. (50")

The Dogon call this type of mask *satimbe* and use it in performances of the men's *awa* mask society to honor deceased elders at the *dama* death anniversary ceremonies. The mask represents the *Yasigine*, the only woman in the village who is allowed to participate in the *awa*. "Satimbe in Dogon means 'Sister of the head.' The mask represents not only the first *Yasigine* ('sister of the *sigui*'), but also all subsequent women who are *Yasigine*. Women become *Yasigine* if they are born during the *sigui* ceremony and display unusual social behavior, or if they demonstrate spirit possession, regardless of whether or not they were born during *sigui*. Some women who are sterile or cannot have male offspring attribute these problems to a violation of taboos and espouse spirit possession as a means of dealing with the problems. They are also *Yasigine*" (Imperato 1984).

Unlike other female mask characters which are represented by fiber masks, the *satimbe* is always made of wood. Its dance is described as "visually pleasing and calm" (DeMott 1982:111).

This mask should be compared with the Mossi *karan-wemba* mask. Both stem from the same tradition, for the ancestors of the Mossi who carved the *karan-wemba* were Dogon. Five hundred years of divergent stylistic development have resulted in a number of important style differences, especially in the shape of the mask face, which is oval among the Mossi and rectangular among the Dogon. In addition, Dogon masks show strong influences of the Mandé style, especially in the conical breasts projecting from flat, rectilinear shoulders. Both styles share the use of red, white and black painted geometric patterns, which are quite typical of all of the sculpture of the Upper Volta River Basin.

19. BWA, Burkina Faso / Mask / Wood / H. 250.2 cm. (98")

In most of the literature written before about 1970 on African art, masks in this style and of this type were misattributed to the Bobo-Fing. The reason is that the Bwa have borrowed many of their cultural traditions from neighboring ethnic groups, especially the Bobo-Fing, Ko, and Nuna. When questioned by early French ethnographers, the Bwa initially identified themselves as Bobo, and only when pressed, did they state that they were different from the Bobo in many ways and should correctly be called Bwa.

One of the cultural elements borrowed from the Nuna, who live to the northeast, is the tradition of carving wooden masks and decorating them with red, white, and black geometric patterns. The most spectacular of the masks adopted by the Bwa are the great plank masks used in several southern Bwa villages, especially Boni, Dossi, and Pa. The Bwa in other areas, especially near the northern border between Mali and Burkina Faso, do not use plank masks, or wooden masks of any type or style.

Yet in the south, plank masks appear at several occasions throughout the year. The primary season for mask performances is from early March to early May, when the rains begin. Masks are used in funerals to honor the deceased, and in the initiations of young men and women into the secrets of mask performances. They are also used in an annual renewal rite to cleanse the village of malevolent forces.

There has been much speculation in the literature about the meanings associated with mask shapes and patterns. According to the Bwa, the hook shape that protrudes from the face is the nose; the crescent at the top of the plank is the moon; and the checkerboard patterns represent the separation of good from evil, wise from stupid, male from female, dark from light.

20. MOSSI, Burkina Faso / Mask, *karan-wemba* / Wood, metal eyes / H. 66.7 cm. (26″)

The Mossi states were founded in about 1500 when a group of horsemen from northern Ghana rode into the basin of the White Volta River and conquered a number of small farmer groups. In the north, in the Yatenga area of Upper Volta, around the city of Ouahigouya, the horsemen encountered the Dogon, who fled to the Bandiagara cliffs. Those Dogon who remained behind were amalgamated into a new Mossi society, but their descendants continue to use masks like this one, very similar in style to the *satimbe* masks used by the modern Dogon to the northwest.

This mask was carved to appear at the funeral of an elderly Mossi woman called a *wemba*, a widow whose children have grown to adulthood, and who returns to her father's household with the rank of a living ancestress—a direct line to the spirits of the family ancestors. The mask represents the woman at the height of her physical beauty, the time just after the birth of her first child when scarification is traditionally applied in patterns radiating from the umbilicus.

This is one of at least eight masks or mask fragments in this same style now held in American and European collections. Well-known examples are in the collections of the late Catherine White in Seattle, the Metropolitan Museum of Art in New York, the Barbier-Mueller Collection in Geneva, and the University Museum at the University of Pennsylvania.

21. NUNA, Burkina Faso / Mask, *koan* / Wood / H. 56.6 cm. (22¼")

Several groups in the area of the upper Volta River basin share the use of red, white and black geometric patterns. Among these are the southwestern Mossi, Bwa, Marka Dafing, Samo, and various "Gurunsi" groups including the Ko, Lela and Nuna. These last three are key to understanding the sculptural styles of the area, for they are probably the originators of the style. The ancestors of the southwestern Mossi, in the area around Koudougou and Ouagadougou were Lela, Nuna and Ko. The Marka Dafing and Samo who moved into the region bringing mask traditions with them were heavily influenced by the styles of the Ko and Nuna, and finally, the Bwa have purchased Ko and Nuna masks like this one outright from their eastern neighbors. As a result, it is virtually im-

possible to distinguish between the styles of many Bwa and Nuna masks.

This mask, from the Nuna village of Tigan, between Koudougou and Dedougou, represents a large female Koba antelope and is called *koan*. As is true throughout Burkina Faso, such masks represent protective spirits from the bush, always closely associated with the spirits of ancestors, and which can take human, animal or even monstrous characteristics. Such masks can perform on several occasions during the dry season from October to May, but they chiefly appear at the funerals of elders and at annual village cleansing ceremonies, when malevolent supernatural spirits are chased from the village.

22., 23. LOBI, Burkina Faso / Figure pair, *bateba* / Wood / H. 64 cm. (25")

Since these beautiful figures were first published in the 1979 catalogue of the Stanley Collection, important research has been carried out among the Lobi by a representative of the Museum Rietberg Zurich, Piet Meyer, who published his work in 1981 in an exhibition catalogue of Lobi art. Such figures are called *bateba*, and serve as intermediaries between protective spirits, *Thila*, and men. The *bateba* belong to *Thila* and can carry out their orders—by holding out an arm to prevent the entrance of evil into the household, or by flying through the night to warn of danger. "The objects defend the territory against evil intruders like witches and sorcerers. Their jurisdiction of the shrine on which they are placed extends generally to the house of the extended family" (Meyer 1984).

Meyer states clearly that in Wourbira, where he carried out most of his research, *bateba* do not represent ancestors, but he also noted that, according to other scholars, around Kampti, they can represent "returned people" who died several generations back. I myself have found that, in the Gaoua area, northeast of Kampti, *bateba* are always associated with ancestral spirits. It seems quite clear the traditions of meaning vary considerably throughout Lobi country, and that it is impossible to generalize. However, whether the spirits in question are ancestral or not, it appears generally true that their function is to protect their owners from harm.

Piet Meyer writes: "As big statues like these were often carved in pairs of male/female figures, we may someday find the two female figures that originally accompanied these two males" (Meyer 1984).

24. BAGA, Guinea / Female figure / Wood / H. 67 cm. (26″)

The Baga are a coastal people (population about 60,000) who live in the transitional area between the Western Sudan, to the northeast, and the Western Guinea Coast, to the southeast. They cultivate rice and have been traditionally governed by the *Simo* society, whose activities, including initiations of young men and the funerals of elder members, primarily take place during the dry season following the harvest.

Objects such as these, in the style of the famous *nimba* masks of the Baga, were placed in male/female pairs in small thatched huts between the village and the forest. They watched over the village and provided both human and agri-cultural fertility (van Geertruyen 1976 and 1979). The figure combines stylistic elements from the Sudan and the Guinea Coast: The C-shaped ear, semi-circular head, and arrow-shaped nose are similar to patterns found on Dogon, Bamana and Mossi sculpture, while the naturalistic, fully rounded body is more characteristic of coastal styles, especially of the Mende, to the southeast.

The object was collected by Emil Storrer in Guinea in 1952 and is illustrated in Hans Himmelheber's study of African art (Himmelheber 1960: 127).

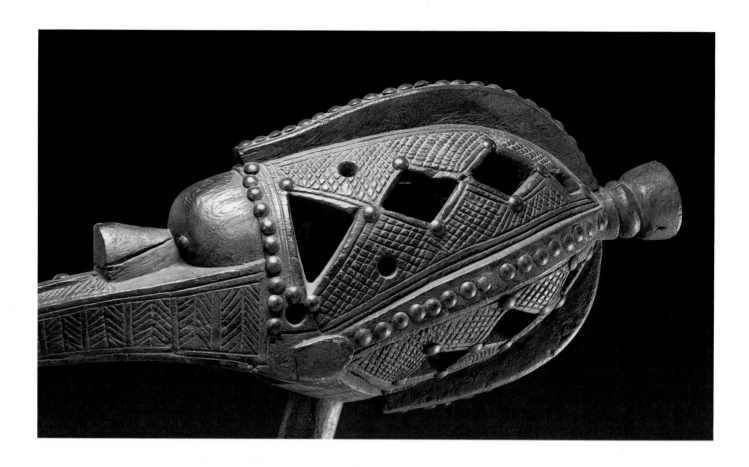

25. BAGA, Guinea / Shrine object, *elek* / Wood, brass upholstery tacks / L. 80 cm. (31")

The Baga place *elek*, objects like this one, on shrines which are symbols of the lineage and which protect the family from malevolent forces. Denise Paulme has written: "In each family house where the eldest member of the lineage resides, a dark corner is reserved for the *elekel* shrine, which is reinvigorated periodically with sacrificial blood . . . A basket protects the whole assemblage. Next to, or on top of, the basket is the *elek* sculpture embodying the ensemble that bears its name. The tutelary (protective) role of the *elek* explains the presence of holes in the head: horns filled with magic powders and unguents, usually kept in the basket, were attached there . . . The *elek* was present at funerals of

family heads, adult members of the group, neighbors, allies, and all other important persons. To say that the *elek* represented the lineage on these occasions is insufficient; it was at once the protector of the group and its most visible sign. It incarnated in some sense the life of the lineage" (Paulme in Vogel 1981:58).

The figure combines animal features—the long beak of a wading bird or the long jaws of a crocodile—with human features, a broad nose and a convex forehead. The elongated skull is pierced with holes to receive horns filled with magical materials. The head is supported by a thin neck which can be removed from its socket in the base.

GUINEA COAST

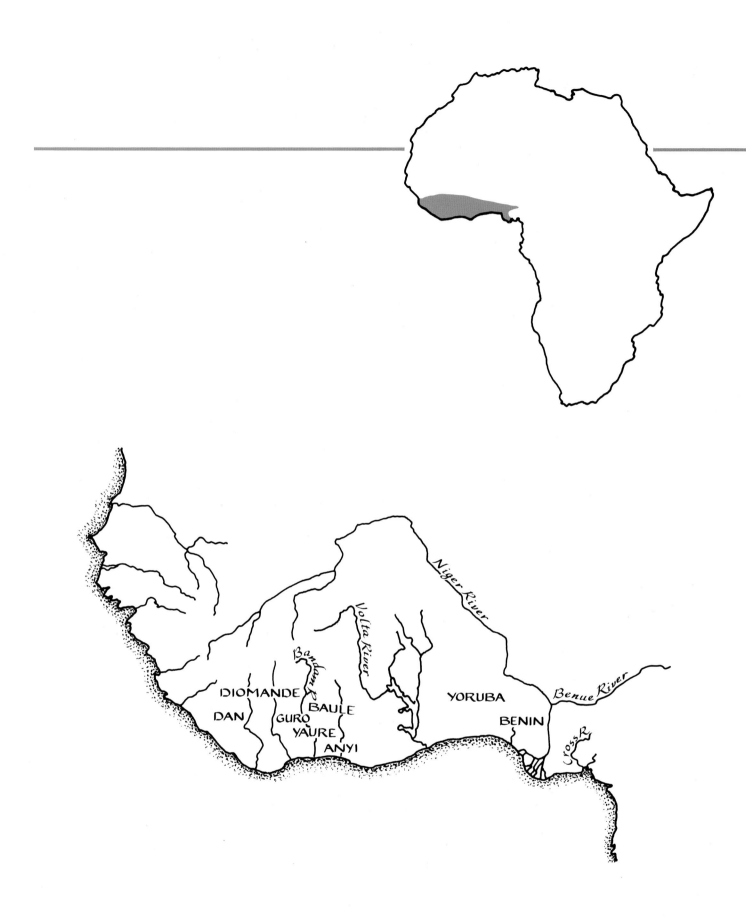

DIOMANDE

DAN

GURO

BAULE

YAURE

ANYI

YORUBA

BENIN

Bandama River

Volta River

Niger River

Benue River

Cross R.

The Guinea Coast Style Area

The Guinea Coast, an area of dense forest interspersed with occasional savannah parklands, stretches along the Gulf of Guinea from the Casamance River north of Bissau to the Niger River delta. In the region of eastern Ghana, Togo, and Benin a broad belt of dry grasslands reaches south to the sea. The Guinea Coast can be divided into two major culture areas, the dividing line following approximately the Bandama River which flows north to south through central Ivory Coast: West of the Bandama, many groups speak Mandé languages and share a history of migration toward the coast from the Mandé heartland at the headwaters of the Niger River. East of the Bandama River, groups speak languages that belong to the Kwa subfamily of languages.

In the west the major subsistence crop is rice, although coconuts, oil palms, and groundnuts are also important. In the east the major crops have been root crops, especially yams, taro, and manioc. Oil palms are important, too, however. The sap of the male bud of the toddy palm is tapped for palm wine, a staple of social and ritual life.

The societies of the western Guinea Coast have generally been non-centralized, fragmentary political groups, in which decisions were made on behalf of the community by councils of elder men. In many areas masks served as agents of social control, enforcing the rules established by the elders. In this area masks also were active in the initiation of young men and women. For example, the Mende *bundu*-spirit helmet masks were worn by middle-aged women to celebrate the entrance of younger women into adult society. From the Mano River west, groups that include the Toma, Bandi, Kpelli, and Kissi use masks in the context of the men's *poro* society, especially for the initiation of young men. Between the Mano and Cavalla Rivers, the Mano, Grebo, Wee, Guro, Bete, and Dan peoples do not have *poro* societies. There, masks appear to entertain, to lead initiation camps, to honor the dead at funerals, and for a number of other events.

In contrast to the politically non-centralized west, the eastern Guinea Coast was notable for the many well-organized, carefully structured bureaucratic states whose power and influence spread over large areas. The Baule and Ashanti king-doms rose to power in the early eighteenth century and were only subjugated by the French and English at the end of the nineteenth century. The great Yoruba city-states of south-western Nigeria flourished in the eighteenth and nineteenth centuries. As early as the thirteenth century, the Yoruba holy city of Ife produced a culture famous for the casting of naturalistic bronze heads, and when the Portuguese visited Benin City in the late fifteenth century, they were much impressed by the magnificence of the *Oba*'s palace, decorated with cast bronze plaques depicting court scenes. Much of the art produced in the eastern Guinea Coast was intended to express the power and wealth of individual rulers and of the state. The Ashanti and Baule are especially famous for their leadership regalia.

It is easier to characterize the art of the western and eastern Guinea Coast in terms of function than style. In the far west, Mandé-speaking groups produce objects that recall the spare, dry forms of the Western Sudan, and that are similarly painted with bright red, white, and black patterns. Masks incorporate the powerful forms of several animals. As we move farther east, figures become increasingly naturalistic and fully rounded, their rich, sensuous black surfaces textured with raised scarification patterns and elaborate hairstyles represented in careful detail. One common characteristic that occurs all along the coast is the depiction of rings of fat around the neck, symbolizing health, prosperity, and well-being.

Beginning in the late fifteenth century, groups living along the Guinea Coast came in contact with Portuguese, French, German, Danish, English, and, later, American merchants and soldiers. Many of the coastal groups, especially the Kru, Fanti, and Ijaw, served as middle-men in the trade between the coast and the interior, and some quickly saw the value of the new materials and techniques the white men brought. They adopted what they valued, and incorporated new forms into old cultural traditions. Much of the art of the Guinea Coast has evolved rapidly to reflect the changing economic and social environment resulting from contact with European culture.

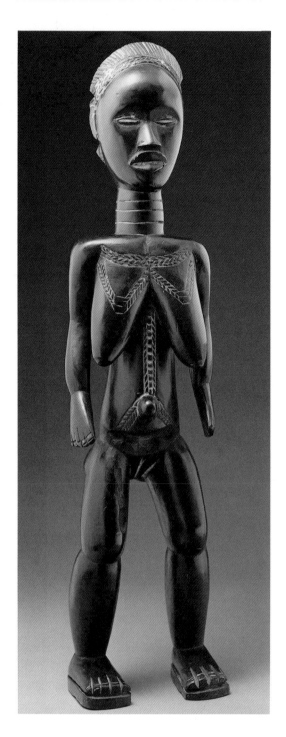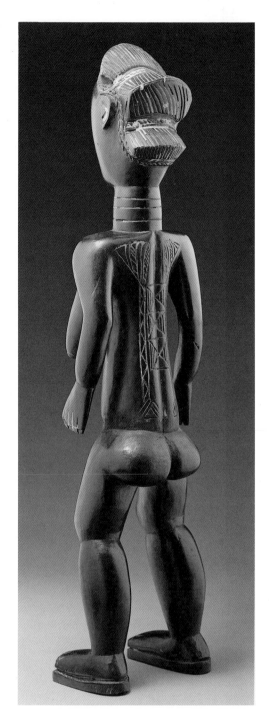

26. DAN, Liberia / Female figure, *lü me* / Wood / H. 69.2 cm. (27″)

The Dan produce large wooden, naturalistic female figures called *lü me*, "wooden person." Such figures, which may be stored in miniature huts built expressly for them, are neither ancestor figures nor representations of spirits, but are intended to be accurate portraits of living people whose names they bear. For example, a wealthy man may commission a portrait of his senior wife, sometimes with a child on her back. Later, when the man gives a large feast at his figure's public unveiling, he will acquire much prestige (Fischer 1984:117–9).

This figure's hairstyle is typical of the Nquäa Dan who live in the border area between the Dan and the western We or Kran. The hair's plaited complexity, as well as the rings of fat around the neck, the heavy, sagging breasts, and the elaborate scarification patterns, is a highly appreciated mark of Dan female beauty.

27. DAN, Liberia / Mask, *tankagle* / Wood / H. 24.1 cm. (9½″)

The Dan believe that the world is animated by a force called *dü*. This force is manifested as invisible spirits that may take human or animal form, and may be made tangible through the carving of a mask. The mask spirits are thought to live in the mountains. "In these remote areas, on the high cliffs still surrounded by virgin forest, there exists a kingdom where no man has penetrated, the place where mask *dü* live out their spiritual existence." The spirits manifest themselves through the masks. They wish to instruct and to help mankind, and make their wishes known through the dreams of men. Each

masquerade has a praise-name or title that explains its function (Fischer 1984:6–9,23).

This mask belongs to the type called *tankagle*, the entertainment masquerade. Its slit eyes are considered feminine characteristics. The mask was worn with a fabric cape, an enormous fiber skirt, and a bonnet-like *komo* cap decorated with cowrie shells or colored glass beads and sometimes bone hairpins taken from women in the audience and thrust into the cap.

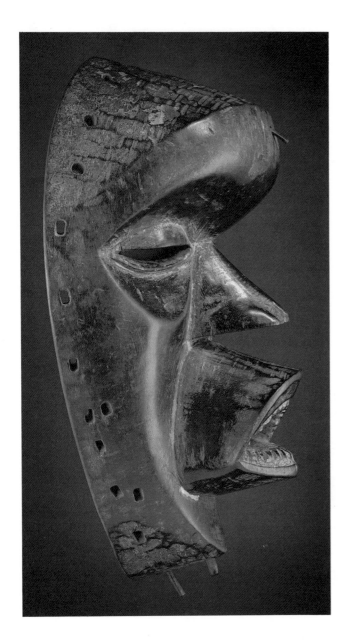
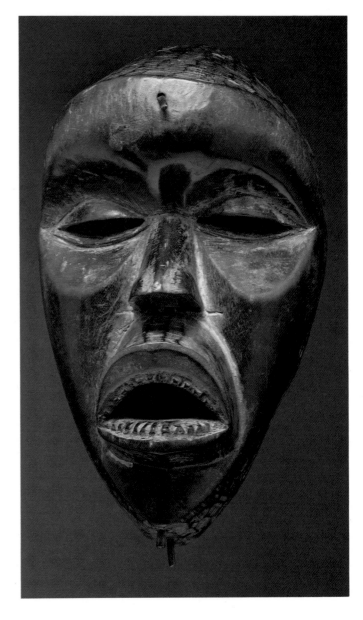

28. DAN, Liberia / Mask, *tankagle* / Wood, metal / H. 19.4 cm. (7⅝″)

Like the previous example, this mask was used in the *tankagle* masquerade of the Dan. *Tankagle* means "dancing, miming masquerade"; the masks entertain the villagers. "These characters may appear with an orchestra and a chorus, or with a single attendant, *gekie*. They carry calabash rattles, and like unmasked dancers, usually wear leg rattles as well. They entertain the spectators with various beautiful dances, and sometimes they perform short skits or songs" (Fischer 1984:23).

In disagreement with most of the notes published in earlier popular studies of African masks, it should be pointed out

that neither this nor other Dan mask types is associated with the *poro*, the international initiation society found among other groups in Liberia and Sierra Leone. Neither the Dan nor the nearby We (Gere) and Mano have the *poro*. The *poro* is a hierarchical society in which every man has a rank corresponding to his qualifications for admission. Dan society is far more democratic and egalitarian, and there is no segregation in the circumcision camp based on social status (Fischer 1984:103).

29. DAN, Liberia and Ivory Coast / Ladle, *wakemia* / Wood, metal / H. 64.8 cm. (25")

The Dan carve large spoons called *wakemia* or *wunkirmian*, "spoon associated with feasts," that are carried by the most hospitable woman (*wakede*, called *wunkirle* in other reports) in a village neighborhood. "A *wakede* must be successful and industrious, and well accomplished in farming. She is the woman in her household who is responsible for the administration of food resources for the entire extended family. She must be of a generous and liberal disposition, a woman who gladly offers her hospitality to anyone at any time. She must provide food and lodging for guests; she must invite travelling musicians or other groups who are passing through the village to eat in her home . . . In order to be able to achieve all this,

the *wakede*, not surprisingly, needs the help of a spirit which incarnates as her large spoon—just as [Dan] mask spirits are incarnated in face masks. The spoon-spirits are believed to animate the *wakemia* to the extent that it may move itself without human assistance" (Fischer 1984 : 124).

In many cases the handles of these spoons are carved to represent their owners at the height of physical beauty and fertility. The bowls of the ladles represent the belly, "pregnant with rice." Frequently, ladle in hand, the *wakede* dances through the neighborhood giving out bowls of rice or small coins to those she meets.

30. DIOMANDÉ, Ivory Coast / Mask / Wood, cloth, shell, metal, feathers / H. 64.1 cm. (25")

The Diomandé are a subgroup of the Mandé-speaking Mau, and are listed by George Murdock as one of the "Nuclear Mandé" groups who share many cultural patterns with Mandé-speakers to the north, including the Bamana, Kasonke, Soninke, and Malinke. Their masks are virtually indistinguishable from those of the Dan, and seem to conform to Dan patterns of use and meaning.

Both the crest of feathers and the long curving beak indicate that this belongs to the bird mask type which the Dan call *gegon*. Eberhard Fischer suggests that the Mau beaked mask type may have influenced the Dan *gegon* (Fischer 1984 : 82). Among the Dan, the masquerade mimes the movements of a bird and sings a song about the toucan—one of the first beings

created and the one that brought palm nuts and the oil palm to the region. "This conception of the toucan as an exceptional being, is widely held throughout West Africa, but among the western Dan it is rare that the idea is given a visual expression as a masquerade. This suggests that although *gegon* is merely an entertainer for the northern Dan today, at one time, the songs, dance sequences and proverbs probably filled a genuinely instructive role. This idea is supported by the *guese* masquerades which have been recorded in nearby Man. These masks, which are formally related to the *gegon*, with the characteristic beak and beard, are the supreme authority of the Man initiation camp" (Fischer 1984 : 83,85).

31. GURO, Ivory Coast / Mask, *zamlé (zamblé)* / Wood / H. 43.2 cm. (17")

Not only the human, but also the animal masks share these elaborate hairline patterns—one of the distinctive traits of the Guro style. Guro *zamlé* masks are among the most elegant stylizations of animal forms in African art. This mask is unusual for the separation of the tongue from the lower jaw.

Although I have never seen a *zamlé* mask perform in Ivory Coast, in 1977 I attended a funeral in the Mossi village of Lemeséré, east of Yako in northern Burkina Faso, and one of these masks appeared, together with sixteen other masks in the Mossi style. For decades, young Mossi farmers have taken the train from Ouagadougou to Ivory Coast to work on cocoa plantations and on the docks in Abidjan. When a young man from Lemeséré returned home one year with a *zamlé* mask that he had purchased from a Guro carver, his clan repainted it with the traditional Mossi red, white, and black, attached a black fiber costume (*bindu*), and renamed it *katré* (hyena), after the totem of their clan. This seems to be a particularly good illustration of René Bravmann's idea of "Open Frontiers" in the exchange of art between ethnic groups.

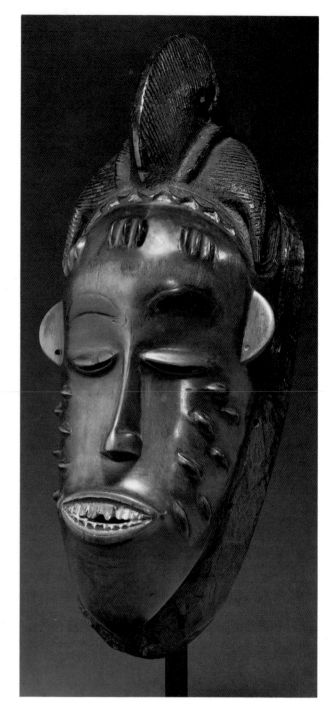

32. GURO, Ivory Coast / Mask / Wood / H. 31.2 cm. (12½″)

The Guro are listed among the "Peripheral Mandé" by George Murdock, and share many cultural characteristics with their Mandé-speaking neighbors to the west and northwest—the Dan, Mende, Vai and Toma. The Guro sculptural style has also often been linked with the style of the Baule, who are their eastern neighbors, but it seems quite clear that it is the Guro who have influenced the Baule, who originated in an area in which very few masks of any style are carved. Field research currently being carried out by Lorenz Homburger

and Eberhard Fischer will soon provide the first useful information about the meaning and function of Guro sculpture.

This female mask wears an elaborate, crested hairstyle with small locks above the ears, and a zig-zagged hairline. Both the high, domed forehead and the cheeks are marked by high-relief scarification patterns, while the open mouth exposes carefully chipped teeth—all this in accordance with Guro fashion.

33. YAURE, Ivory Coast / Mask / Wood / H. 33 cm. (13")

Masks carved by groups in the central portion of the Ivory Coast (including the Baule, Guro, and Yaure) share delicate details of scarification and hairstyle, carefully marked hairlines forming points at the temples, very refined and polished heart-shaped faces with elegantly curving eyebrows, and fine coiffed beards. Because the best-known of these masks are produced by the Baule, it has often been assumed that they originated the style and influenced the Guro and the Yaure, who have been described as close relatives of the Baule (Fagg 1980:60, 61).

In fact, the Guro and the Yaure, who live to the west and southwest of the Baule, are Mandé-speakers whose cultural and artistic patterns are closely related to those of groups to the west in the *poro* area of western Ivory Coast and Liberia. The Baule, who speak an Akan language unrelated to the languages of their western neighbors, and who come from a culture area in which masks are quite rare, seem to have adopted the mask styles of their many neighbors when they penetrated the central Ivory Coast from the east. Thus, it seems very likely that the Baule have been influenced by the Yaure and the Guro, rather than the opposite.

The delicate beauty of this mask is enhanced by the curving, horn-like plaits of hair, which also appear, sometimes combined with pairs of upward curving horns, on many other Yaure masks. The stylized fringe of beard is one of the most common Yaure style characteristics.

34. ANYI, Ivory Coast / Funerary head, *mma* / Fired clay / H. 18.3 cm. (7½")

Among the Sanwi subgroup of the Anyi near Krinjabo, and other groups in southern Ivory Coast and Ghana, fired clay figures and heads served to commemorate deceased men and women. The *mma* figures were considered portraits of the dead, with distinctive scars, hairstyles, beards, hats, jewelry, and other identifying characteristics carefully reproduced. A female potter who had known the deceased modelled the figure and then stained it black and dressed it the day before the final funeral rites. The spirit of the deceased was invited to occupy the *mma*, and then it was deposited, with many other older figurines, in a special clearing in the forest (*mmasso*). The figure was a concrete means of remembering the dead, a resting place for his soul. The figures could also encourage fertility in sterile women who tended the forest clearing and offered yam and manioc. The use of commem-

orative figures was, at first, restricted to nobility, but was later extended to any Sanwi—except children (Amon d'Aby 1960:67 and Vogel 1981:78–79).

This head bears the distinctive protuberant eyes with a deep horizontal slash that are characteristic of the Anyi style. The nose is extremely fine and thin, and the hairstyle is quite complex, consisting of several wedge-shapes that flare outward from the center of the skull. The most remarkable feature is the intricate, colorful pattern of lines that remains on the cheeks and forehead; it was painted on after the head was fired.

There is a fine color photograph of the head in the catalogue of the de Havenon collection at the Museum of African Art in Washington (de Havenon 1971:no. 122).

35. BAULE, Ivory Coast / Couple / Wood / H. 39 cm. (15″)

The Baule carve two important types of anthropomorphic figures. "Spirit spouses" represent the "spouse that everyone had in the other world before he or she was born into this one," and may, therefore, be either male or female. "Other figures, less numerous than these, are carved for nature spirits (*asie usu*) that possess or follow a person and disrupt his or her life until a shrine has been made and a private cult established . . . Baule informants felt that figures carved for nature spirits were more varied than those carved for spirit spouses" (Vogel 1981 : 73). Susan Vogel carried a photograph of this object to Ivory Coast and showed it to informants during her last research trip. The Baule agreed that the couple must represent nature spirits, and that in such cases it is quite the norm for the female figure to be larger than the male.

The male and female figures are seated side-by-side on Akan-style stools, their arms draped around each other's torsos so that, when viewed from the front, they initially appear to have too many hands. Their bodies are quite still and formal, but at the same time supple and sensuous. The elegant lines of the heart-shaped faces, turned just slightly away from each other, are most striking when seen in profile, which emphasizes the sharp details of the ornate hairstyles.

36. BAULE, Ivory Coast / Mask / Wood, fiber / H. 23.8 cm. (10″)

Small Baule face masks like this one (and its female counterpart, not exhibited) are worn in *Goli* dances, entertainment dances which the Baule borrowed from their Mandé-speaking neighbors, the Wan. These dances are performed to celebrate harvests, to commemorate the visits of dignitaries, and at the funerals of male elders, to honor the deceased. Although new characters, steps, and music are occasionally introduced, these performances adhere to a common pattern. "Masks representing domestic and hunted animals, known individuals, and such general types as 'the slave,' 'the prostitute,' 'the dandy,' 'sun,' and 'rainbow' appear one at a time in a series of skits that mime village life." The masks appear one after the other in order of increasing importance, beginning with the ones that represent animals. When not in use, the masks are stored in the village. For dances, they are worn with cloth costumes over raffia skirts. A ram-skin cape, attached to the rear of the mask, covers the performer's back.

This very naturalistic mask, with its carefully plaited beard and elaborate hairstyle, was intended to be a portrait of a character in the village, who would himself appear to dance alongside the masked dancer representing him. Male and female pairs of portrait masks may be colored red and black, and although neither sex is associated consistently with a particular color, red is considered the more beautiful skin color and is associated with purity and competence (Vogel 1977:124–51; 1981:75–7).

37. YORUBA (Northern Ekiti), Nigeria / Staff for Eshu, *ogo Elegba* / Wood, indigo dye, beads / H. 41.8 cm. (17")

Although the pantheon of Yoruba *orisha*, or gods, is extraordinarily rich, only one of the *orisha* is depicted in sculpture. Eshu (or often, Elegba), is the trickster, the messenger of the gods, and the god without whom all the other *orisha* would go hungry. When everything is going well in a person's life, it is Eshu who causes mischief, who is the troublemaker, who leads men astray so that they offend the gods and must make sacrifices to set things aright. Shrines are dedicated to Eshu wherever people come into conflict—at crossroads, markets, and at the entrances to Yoruba homes.

Eshu's character is ambiguous and contradictory: Although he is male, he can be represented by male or female figures. He is both a capricious and mischievous young boy and a wise and reflective old man: "His age is reflected in his cunning

and the wisdom concealed in his trickery, his extreme youth in his wantonness and caprice and in his impulsive behaviour" (Wescott 1962:341). This contradictory nature is expressed more clearly in this staff than in any other Eshu cult object I have seen. Eshu is shown as a young boy blowing a wooden whistle, an act of defiance of established authority. Facing in the opposite direction is the wrinkled face of a wise old man. The two heads are joined by a common hairstyle, drawn up into a long phallic knot. Among the Yoruba, long hair is symbolic of excess libidinous energy and unrestrained sexuality (Wescott 1962:348).

John Pemberton has attributed the staff to the northern part of Ekiti province (Pemberton 1984).

38. YORUBA, Popular Republic of Benin / Mask, for *Efe/Gelede* / Wood / L. 27 cm. (11″)

The *Efe/Gelede* masquerades of the Yoruba of western Nigeria and Benin (formerly Dahomey) are held during the period from March to May at the beginning of the new agricultural season. The performances honor "our mothers," *awon iya wa* and acknowledge the power and authority (*ashe*) of women, whether elderly, ancestral, or deified, in a male-oriented society. "The *ashe* of woman is manifest in the mystery of birth and in the dreadful work of witchcraft. It is a power that cannot be directly observed or controlled, a cool power, de-tected, yet hidden, in the beauty of the composed face" (Fagg and Pemberton 1982 : 56,110).

The work of the artist who created this thin, beautifully carved old piece can be identified by the characteristic shape of the ear. Other masks by the same artist are illustrated in the catalogue of an exhibition of Yoruba sculpture held in New York in 1982 (Fagg and Pemberton 1982:plates 2,5,29,49). These objects were carved in the Anago or Ifonyin area of Benin, perhaps in the nineteenth century (Drewal 1984).

39. YORUBA (Eastern, Owo), Nigeria / Divination tapper, *iroke Ifa* / Ivory / H. 25.1 cm. (10")

When a Yoruba is beset by problems or faced with an important decision he may consult a diviner, called *babalawo*, "father of the secret," who makes known the will of the gods, especially Olorun, god of destiny and father of all the Yoruba *orisha*. The diviner sits facing his client, a dust-covered wooden tray between them. His left hand rests on an *agere Ifa*, a bowl that contains the sixteen palm-nuts cast in the divination process. His right hand may hold an *iroke Ifa*, like this one, that he strikes lightly against the edge of the tray to invoke Orunmila, to call his attention.

The style of this object is quite similar to a group of objects, many in ivory, that William Fagg has attributed to the city of Owo, in the eastern Yoruba area, north of Benin City. Much Owo sculpture was produced for trade with Benin, and Henry Drewal has pointed out that the style and especially the scarification over the eyes, on the torso and thighs, is closer to Edo/Benin than to Yoruba (Drewal 1984).

40., 41. YORUBA (Oyo, Erin/Ilobu/Oshogbo area), Nigeria / Figure pair / Wood, beads / H. 53.3, 51.4 cm. (21, 20¼")

This male/female pair was intended for the shrine of one of the many Yoruba *orisha* (deities), to honor the god and to remind supplicants of the blessings their devotion could bring. Female figures are often represented holding a bowl, and carrying a child on the back, or, as in this example, nursing an infant. "A statue of a woman and child, usually called a maternity figure, personifies fertility and the continuity of life. It was placed on an altar in a shrine or sanctuary" (Walker in Vogel 1981:108). Male figures are often depicted riding a horse or donkey, a symbol of power and aggression. "Equestrian motifs on houseposts and door panels have been described as depictions of the invaders of northeastern Yorubaland, an area that was overrun by Benin from the southeast, Oyo and later Ibadan from the west, and Nupe and Ilorin from the north" (Ojo in Vogel 1981:117).

Henry Drewal has noted that the style of the pair, the ears and head position as well as the treatment of the arms, suggests the Maku School at Erin. He based this judgement on the similarity of this figure pair to objects attributed to Maku of Erin by Fagg (1982:40–41, fig. 45) and by himself (1980:61, especially nos. 96, 97).

42., 43. YORUBA (Egba, Abeokuta), Nigeria / Twin figures, *ere ibeji* / Wood, beads / H. 20 cm. (8″)

The Yoruba have one of the highest rates of twin births in the world (45 per 1000 births). The birth of twins is an occasion to celebrate, but it is also cause for concern, for twins can bring their parents good fortune or great trouble. Because twins are more fragile at birth than single births, frequently one or both infants may die. If one twin dies, the parents consult a diviner, the *babalawo*, who may indicate that an *ere ibeji* must be carved. While the figure is being carved, the mother sends gifts of food to the artist; she will present additional gifts when the carving is completed. "Upon receiving the figure from the carver, she will place it on her back tucked within her wrapper as she would a living child, and dance to her house, hearing all the way the songs for *ibeji* sung by the women of her compound" (Pemberton in Fagg and Pemberton 1982 : 162). The figure is placed on a small shrine in the mother's sleeping room, its face is washed, and it is dressed in rich garments and beads. The figure may be fed the

favorite foods of twins, beans and palm oil. Its body is rubbed with red camwood powder and oil, its hair with dark indigo dye. It may be put to bed at night with a blanket to keep it warm in the cold harmattan season. If the *ibeji* figure is honored in these ways, the spirit of the deceased infant may bring its parents wealth and good luck.

This pair represents two deceased female infants. The identical patterns of wear and similarities in the use of beads indicate that they were carved at the same time for one family. They are quite obviously by the same artist, from the Egba Yoruba city of Abeokuta. They appear to have been carved by a member of the school of Esubiyi, Itoko quarter, established by Egbado immigrants in the 1860's. They may be the work of Akiode, who died in 1936 (Drewal 1980: 53). They are by the same hand as a male/female pair illustrated in Stoll 1980, page 118, no. 12.

44. YORUBA (Ijebu), Nigeria / Face bell, *omo* / Bronze / H. 19.7 cm. (7⅔")

Bronze face bells are used as symbols of power and leadership among the southern Ijebu Yoruba. The bells represent ancient ancestors, and each new chief must have a new face bell cast for his son to wear suspended over the right shoulder and resting against the left hip (Thompson 1970: fig. 16, note 13).

The Ijebu area is one of the most important Yoruba bronze casting centers, perhaps as a result of the acquisition of bronze casting technology from Benin, to the east, before 1700. Contact with Benin has resulted in many similarities in the iconography of cast bronze patterns (Williams 1974: 258–259). John Pemberton has noted that the patterns cast in low relief beneath the chin are similar to Benin castings. He speculates that the three pegs that project from the right side of the head refer to the *Oshugbo* or *Ogboni* secret society, for whom the number three represents stability and the support of mankind by the earth. The presence of the three pegs may indicate that the owner was a member of *Ogboni*, which is particularly powerful in the Ijebu area. "Thus, it would appear that the cult of the Earth and the worship of Onile . . . is intimately related to the concept of ancestors and kingship in the extremely complex Ijebu political and judicial systems" (Pemberton in Fagg and Pemberton 1982: 70, plate 9).

45. YORUBA (Oyo, Erin), Nigeria / Figure for a Shango shrine / Wood / H. 81 cm. (33″)

This figure represents a drummer wearing the hairstyle of a priest of Shango and playing the *bata* drum for the deified king. The *bata* drum is said to have been introduced by Shango to increase his prestige and terrify his opponents. The drum consists of a cylinder of wood with hide membranes stretched across both ends and laced together with cords. Yet unlike similar drums used in the Western Sudan, which are held under the arm, and so can be squeezed to tighten the cords and vary the pitch, the *bata* drum is suspended horizontally by a broad band and is played with both hands. The only change in pitch is produced by muting.

This figure was carved by Toibo of Erin for the Shango shrine of the Timi (ruler) of Ede. Toibo was the son of Maku (d. 1927), the master carver of Erin. Toibo himself died before 1955, when Ulli Beier studied the sculpture in the Shango shrine of the Timi of Ede (1957). John Pemberton has described the characteristics of Toibo's style: "There is the elongated, oval head set diagonally on the slightly curved neck; the line of the chin carried around behind the neck; the stylization of the ear and the hatching below and across the center of the eye; and the powerful, sloping shoulders" (Pemberton in Fagg and Pemberton 1982:54, plate 1).

46. YORUBA, Nigeria / Staff for Shango, *oshe Shango* / Wood / H. 39 cm. (15")

This is a dance wand carried by a devotee of the Yoruba deity Shango. While the devotee dances, the *orisha* (god) possesses his follower's body. Shango was the fourth king of Old Oyo, who was compelled to commit suicide as a result of his misuse of power. After his death, however, his followers declared him to be an *orisha* whose powers are seen in thunder and lightning.

"The female figure with the twin celts or thunderax of Shango, *edan ara*, balanced upon her head is an extraordinary image when seen in the hands of a devotee possessed by the *orisha*. Dancing to the piercing, crackling sounds and staccato rhythms of the *bata* drum, the possessed devotee, the *elegunshango*, will wave the *oshe* with violent and threatening gestures and then, in an instant, draw it to him- or herself in a motion of quiet composure. The thunderbolts, like lightning,

clearly convey the sudden, overwhelming, and seemingly capricious power of Shango" (Pemberton in Fagg and Pemberton 1982 : 74).

This dance wand for Shango was carved in the southwestern Egbado Yoruba area. John Pemberton has suggested that the style of the ears and eyes and the pattern of the coiffure indicate a central or southern Egbado origin. The figure once held a prayer rattle or a tiny representation of an *oshe Shango* in her right hand (now broken off). Over her left shoulder she carries a ritual object which Henry and Margaret Drewal have identified recently as an "emblem of Oya, deity of the Niger River and wife of Shango" (Drewal 1984).

The figure is particularly notable for the great care given to small details, such as the knot of the cloth wrapper and the beautiful patterns of the hairstyle.

47. YORUBA (Ekiti, Efon-Alaye), Nigeria / Helmet mask, *elefon* / Wood / H. 128.9 cm. (51½")

Masks of this type, called *elefon* in Efon-Alaye in northeast Yoruba country, were worn over the head by strong young men in order to memorialize the ancestors of the family that owns the mask. The figures that surmount the pot-shaped mask (*ikoko*) are not intended to be portraits of the dead, but "are idealized presentations of historic personages who are remembered for having embodied in their lifetime culturally recognized values. They are figures of praise and figures to be praised . . . When the mask is danced in joyous processions throughout the town or knelt before in the quiet of a family shrine, the 'presence' of the deceased is acknowledged, and the reality he or she embodied is affirmed and known again in the lives of the celebrants and worshippers. The *iwa*—the 'character,' the moral quality and dignity, the beauty and authority—of the person and his or her life is made manifest through the revealing power of the mask, and praised in dance, song, and prayer through Epa and Elefon" (Pemberton in Fagg and Pemberton 1982 : 132,146).

This *elefon* mask, formerly in the Hooper Collection, has been attributed by William Fagg to a member of the Adeshina family of carvers in Efon-Alaye. The mask may be by Agbon-biofe, who died in 1945, or by "an equally fine unnamed master." A mask by the very same artist, but with a mounted male figure that wears the same crown and beads, is in the Catherine White Collection in Seattle (White 1984 : 82–83).

The female figure wears an impressive conical crown. The object in her right hand is the handle of a fly whisk, and she wears a necklace of large coral beads. All of these are symbols of chieftaincy. Although female chiefs are rare, they do occur in several Yoruba towns. The highest ranking female chief is called *Iyalode*, or "mother of all." She represents the "collective interests of women before the king and in the councils of the senior chiefs, and [has] the authority to take disciplinary action against women who have seriously violated social or political conventions." The figure of a woman, held upside down by her legs, represents the power of the *Iyalode* to discipline women who have gone astray (Pemberton in Fagg and Pemberton 1982 : 146, plate 47; Carroll 1984).

48. YORUBA, Nigeria / Staffs, *edan Ogboni* / Bronze / H. 30 cm. (11″)

Staffs of this type are presented to elder initiates into the *Ogboni* society, a society intended to transcend kinship ties in traditional communities and which held the "power of reconciling and adjudicating differences among persons and atoning for the violation of the earth." The two figures, linked by a chain, refer to the *Ogboni* concept: "Two *Ogboni*, it becomes three . . . The union of male and female in the *edan* image symbolizes this putting two together to make a third" (Morton-Williams in Fagg and Pemberton 1982:186). The female holds a pair of *edan Ogboni*, while the male makes the *Ogboni* salute—left hand above right, thumbs hidden—the sign of greeting to Onile, "owner of the house" (Fagg and Pemberton 1982:186).

This *edan* pair is notable for the brilliance of the bronze caster's technique; he has produced a smooth, flawless surface of great detail. The three-dimensional quality, with arms free of the torso and bent knees projecting outward, is unusual. The protuberant, "keeled" eyes are a style characteristic of objects made for *Ogboni*.

49. BENIN KINGDOM (Edo), Nigeria / Hip pendant, *uhunmwun-ekhue* / Brass / H. 18.4 cm. (7¼")

This pendant was created for the court of the Kingdom of Benin, a highly centralized state founded in the thirteenth or fourteenth century in southwestern Nigeria, which was ruled by a divine king, or Oba, and his complex pyramidal bureaucracy of Palace Chiefs, Town Chiefs, minor palace officials, and members of the guilds. The guilds were composed of craftsmen who produced sculpture in wood, ivory, and brass, embroidered cloths, and other court regalia.

The Portuguese visited Benin in the 1470's, and Duarte Pacheco Pereira described the state: "The Kingdom of Beny [Benin] is about eighty leagues long and forty wide; it is usually at war with its neighbors and takes many captives, whom we buy at twelve or fifteen brass bracelets each, or for copper bracelets which they prize more" (Ben Amos 1980:6,7). In 1897 a British expeditionary force attacked Benin, looted the palace, and burned it. Although the members of the brass casters' guild (*Igun Eronmwon*) continue to cast royal and chiefly regalia today, most of the objects from Benin in collections outside of Nigeria, including this piece, date from the long period before the British attack.

This "mask" was worn by chiefs of all ranks as part of their ceremonial attire, the pendant attached to the bunched cloth of the wrapper on the left hip. "In form it is related to the brass pendant masks sent to vassal rulers . . . and the ivory pendant mask worn by the Oba" (Ben Amos 1980:75 and 1984).

The head is represented wearing a crown made largely of pink fire-coral beads. The decorative pattern beneath the chin represents a row of mud fish—some cast in brass as part of the whole head, some cast in a different alloy of copper. Thus, when the object was polished, a clear pattern of alternating colors emerged. The strip down the nose is copper; the pupils of the eyes are iron. Both these details were made first, then set into the wax model before the brass was poured—this again to create a color contrast.

The stylization of the ear, nostrils, and especially the full and sensuous lips seems to indicate a date in the first half of the nineteenth century.

EQUATORIAL FOREST

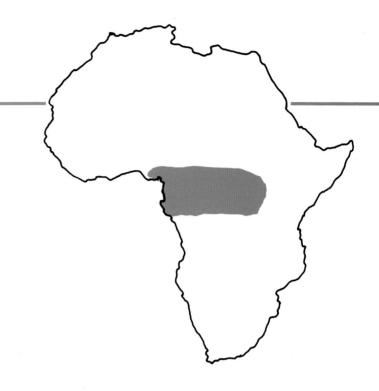

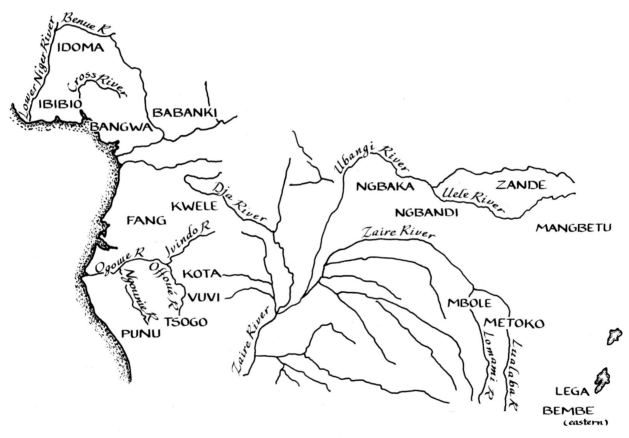

The Equatorial Forest Style Area

The Equatorial Forest lies north and south of the equator from the Niger River delta to Lake Tanganyika. This is the surprisingly small portion of Africa that corresponds to the stereotyped image of dense jungle dripping with moisture, and small communities in isolated forest clearings. The region is by no means uniformly flat and featureless, however, for there are great mountains in Cameroon and Gabon, and mighty rivers, including the Ogowe and Ngounié in Gabon, the Uele, Ubangi, and Zaire Rivers in Zaire, and Lakes Edward, Albert, and Kivu in the far east. Broad arms of forest vegetation spread along river systems into the Southern Savannah style area, and there are large areas of open grasslands in Gabon and Congo (Brazzaville). The major crops, planted in clearings opened by slash-and-burn farming, or in the scattered areas of grassland, include corn, cassava, yams, bananas, and oil palms. Much of the dense forest is inhabited by pygmies who hunt and gather honey to trade to farmers for cultivated crops. The migration of Bantu-speaking peoples throughout the area may have followed the introduction of Malaysian food crops—including yams, bananas, and taro—that were suitable for cultivation in the forest.

It is possible to chart correspondences between the distribution of language families and sculptural styles in the Western Sudan and the Guinea Coast, but east of the Niger River this is no longer possible because all groups speak languages in the Benue-Kongo, or Bantu, sub-family of the Niger-Kongo family of languages. This is the result of the dispersion of Bantu-speaking peoples from somewhere in the highland border area between Nigeria and Cameroon throughout the entire southern third of Africa during the past 3000 years. The only non-Bantu groups that produce sculpture are intrusive groups such as the Mangbetu in northeastern Zaire.

Perhaps as a result of low population density and the isolation imposed by the rain forest environment, there are no strongly organized political systems. The largest social groupings have been villages composed of several clans, or in the grasslands of Cameroon, small kingdoms of a few villages. Only the Mangbetu created a large-scale empire in the nineteenth century. The forest was a barrier to long-distance trade and communication, and here, more than anywhere else in Africa, geographical features including river systems and micro-environments such as the Cameroon grasslands, have determined settlement patterns, migration routes, agricultural techniques, and the interchange of sculptural styles.

The major style characteristic that occurs throughout the Equatorial Forest is the white, heart-shaped face, which appears from the Kwele and Vuvi in the west, to the Lega and Bembe in the east. In the valleys of the Ogowe and the Ngounié, masks and figures share the use of delicate black lines to define brows, nose, eyes and mouth. Figures in several very idiosyncratic styles are used in reliquary cults, where they protect the bones of revered ancestors from malevolent forces. In northern Zaire, roughly carved objects were used by societies of indigenous peoples to counter the power of an intrusive political hierarchy; refined, beautifully finished, naturalistic figures were commissioned for the royal court. In the east, the Lega and many related groups use masks and figures in the ceremonies of graded societies.

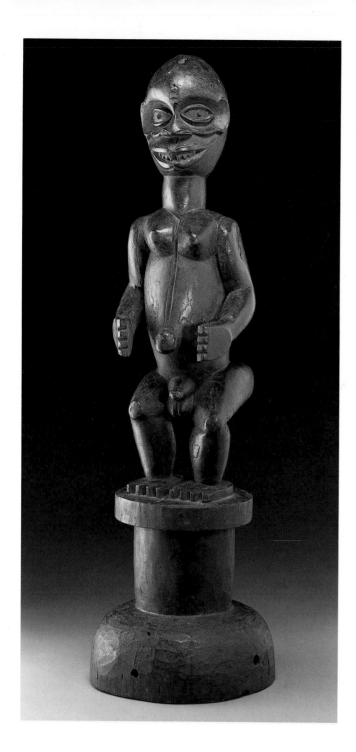

50. IBIBIO (Eket), Nigeria / Male figure / Wood / H. 61 cm. (24″)

That this figure's concave base has been provided with holes indicates that it was used in the *ugbom* (*ogbom*) plays in honor of *Ala*, the earth deity. *Ogbom* "was believed to make children plentiful. It was performed towards the middle of the year on every eighth day for eight weeks by each section of the village in turn. Each section had two carvings. Everyone joined in the dance, but only men wore the headdresses. Their identity was not concealed and they were not considered to be supernatural beings. Compact groups of dancers moved about joyfully and those with headdresses danced singly in the midst in a scene of great excitement" (Murray 1949 : no. 88–

99). G. I. Jones states that the *ugbom* "appears to have been a women's fertility ritual. It was carried aloft on the head of a male bearer who stood in the centre of a ring of dancing and singing women . . . Two rotating wheels festooned with coloured ribbons and streamers were carried fore and aft on a wooden axle, which passed through a hole in the base of the carving" (Jones 1984 : 201–2).

On the basis of style, this male figure has been attributed to the southern Eket subgroup of the Ibibio. The carefully defined features of the face, heavy musculature, and flex-kneed stance are common in Eket style figures (cf. Neyt 1979 : no. 1,2,3).

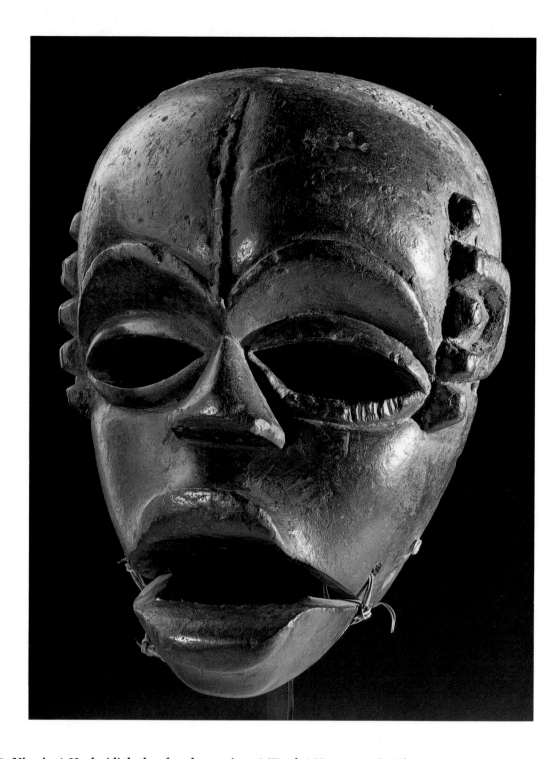

51. IBIBIO, Nigeria / Mask, *idiok ekpo* for *ekpo* society / Wood / H. 24.2 cm. (9½")

Both light-colored, beautiful masks with delicate features, and dark, ugly, frightening masks like this example were used by the Ibibio men's *ekpo* society. "*Ekpo* is a male society that is said to have been captured in the distant past from women. In former times all males belonged to it and its duties were to propitiate the ancestors for the welfare of the community, to uphold the power of the elders and to maintain the social order. Its rituals were secret, and any non-member who witnessed them was killed . . . The masks represent spirits from the underworld" (Murray 1949: nos. 30–48).

There are two major types of *ekpo* masks. Masks of the first type, called *mfon ekpo*, have delicate features—"a narrow, high-bridged nose, thin lips, pointed chin, and high forehead"—and are painted light red, green, yellow and white.

They represent deceased persons who led good moral lives. Masks of the second type, called *idiok ekpo*, like this characteristic piece, have coarse, ugly features, are painted black, brown, and blue, and represent persons whose evil deeds have caused them to become ghosts. The "good" *mfon ekpo* masks appear during the day, and the "evil" *idiok ekpo* masks appear during the night (Messenger 1973 : 121–123).

This mask bears the thick, everted lips, large eyes, heavy scars, bulging forehead, and dark color that the Ibibio associate with evil, malevolent spirits. The lower jaw is articulated so that the dancer could snap it noisily shut during performances. Before he appeared, the performer rubbed his body with charcoal and put on a vest and skirt of long, blackened raffia fibers. Only his darkened arms and legs were bared.

52. IDOMA, Nigeria / Female figure / Wood / H. 92.1 cm. (36″)

This serene and dignified female figure is almost three feet tall. She wears an elaborate crest of feather shapes extending from the forehead to the nape of the neck. Large, rectangular scars arranged in vertical rows of three mark the temples, and a very elaborate system of zig-zag patterns extends from the throat to the umbilicus. She is seated on a cylindrical stool, perhaps indicating high rank. The entire figure is covered with a thick coat of soot from years of smoking above a cooking fire to preserve it from insect damage.

A female figure in a very similar pose was photographed by Roy Sieber in 1958 in Oturkpo-Icho village. It was said to have been placed next to the bodies of old men at their funerals (Sieber 1961:9).

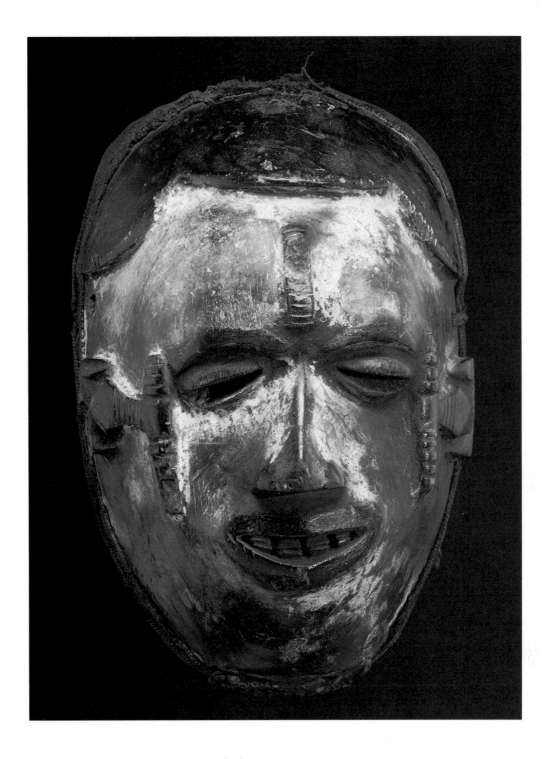

53. IDOMA, Nigeria / Mask / Wood / H. 22.5 cm. (9")

Although this mask lacks the horn-like projections that are characteristic of many Idoma masks, comparison with field photos taken in 1958 by Roy Sieber of masks carved in about 1946 by the Idoma artist Adaba from Otobi village makes it quite certain that the work is, in fact, Idoma and not Ibo. The masks seen by Professor Sieber were identified as *Ichahoho*, which appeared on the day of the dead, during the dry season, but before hunting begins (Sieber 1961:ill. 22 and 1984). Supporting evidence comes from Sidney Kasfir, who states that it is "similar to *Ichahoho* men's society masks but lacks the characteristic horn-like projections. In Idoma it is never possible to be sure of the identity of a white-face mask unless [this information] has been established at the time of collec-tion, because identical masks are sometimes used by different mask societies (of which there are many)." Kasfir attributes the mask to the artist Ochigbo of Awmayi, on the basis of similarities to a mask in the Jos museum—a mask known to have been carved by him (66J.4.132) (Kasfir 1984).

"Idoma white-faced masks are used today [as in 1958] in the usual context of funerals (second burials) of society members, but formerly played an important role in government and law enforcement. *Ichahoho* was a warrior society, and the ex-tremely life-like appearance of the mask is attributable to the fact that it represents the severed head of an enemy" (Kasfir 1984).

54. WESTERN BANGWA, Cameroon / Royal figure / Wood / H. 57 cm. (22½")

Much of the art of the Grasslands area of Cameroon is political art: objects reflect the wealth, power, and prestige of the ruler—the *Fon*—and of the royal family. These leadership objects include pipes, prestige caps, stools, drinking horns, calabashes, necklaces, bracelets, and the figures of royal ancestors. These latter may include male figures of deceased *Fon* and female figures of their wives. All are kept in the royal treasury in the palace and are displayed during leadership ceremonies, including the funerals of the *Fon*, enthronements, and annual festivals.

Pierre Harter has seen objects very similar to this one in the Grasslands: "This is a commemorative statue of a royal princess or *angkweta*, belonging to the *lefem* society of the western Bangwa. I saw the figure of a standing woman, carved by the same artist, during a visit to Fotabong I made in 1967. I saw a lot more of them, also by the same artist, in 1980, in a granary of the palace of Fontem—these objects were offered for sale. It is probable that the artist is still living, but I do not know his name" (Harter 1984).

The figure is seated on a royal stool, and is wearing a crown, and holding leadership symbols, including a calabash in her left hand and a pipe in her right.

55. BABANKI, Cameroon / Figure group / Wood / H. 45 cm. (18")

The palaces of Cameroon Grasslands' chiefs are often decorated with genre figures and figures of members of the royal family, living and dead. This composition of two figures astride a strange-looking plank may have been part of a facade decoration, perhaps surrounding the door to the palace, or it may be a fragment of one of the posts that supported the overhanging thatched roof of the palace. However, the accumulation of a thick layer of soot indicates that the object must have been stored for many years in the rafters of a palace kitchen.

For some time I was unable to understand the meaning of the group. Then I looked beneath the plank on which the figures are seated. Signs of damage at the front and back indicate that the carved wooden wheels of a bicycle have been removed, and that the large figure and its smaller companion were intended to be seen seated on a bicycle or scooter, perhaps of the type illustrated in Tamara Northern's recent catalogue of Grasslands art (Northern 1984 : 141).

56. FANG, southern Cameroon and northern Gabon / Reliquary guardian, *eyima bieri* / Wood, metal / H. 42.5 cm. (17")

The Fang are a numerous and aggressive people who immigrated into southern Cameroon and Gabon during the nineteenth century, and who were reputed for their frequent raids on the villages of neighboring groups, whom they rapidly displaced during their travels south.

The Fang are also famous for their figure sculpture, which is used in the context of ancestral sacrifices of the *bieri* religion. The Fang attach wooden figures and heads to cylindrical bark boxes which contain the skulls and long bones of the important ancestors of the clan. The figures are intended to protect the relics from malevolent forces. During the initiation of male heads of households, the wooden figures may be carried like puppets in exuberant and frolicsome dances while the skulls of the ancestors are displayed and the achievements of each are recited.

James Fernandez has described the pose of these figures as one of ". . . protective benevolence . . . The figures have an air of secret knowledge appropriate to the ancestors. Indeed, Fang folk etymology derives their general term for carved figure, *eyema*, from the root, *yem*, to know" (Fernandez 1975:744).

Louis Perrois has developed a system of style classification based on the proportion of head/neck/torso/legs (a system which Fernandez criticizes for subjective selection and describes as "qualitative quantification"). This figure seems to fit Perrois substyle "equiforme allongé" (elongated equi-form) (Perrois 1972:180–184) and is most similar in the shape of the head, mouth, hairstyle, and shoulders—as well as proportions—to objects he describes as "transitional Ntumu/Ngumba". Thus the object appears to have been carved in the area of southern Cameroon just north of the border with Rio Muni.

The surface of the figure exudes a sticky palm oil which the Fang used to clean the figure before offering sacrifices to ask for the blessings of the ancestors. It holds the tiny figure of an ancestor between its hands.

57. FANG, southern Cameroon, Rio Muni (Equatorial Guinea), northern Gabon / Mask, *ngontang* / Wood / H. 70 cm. (25")

The Fang produce masks with four white faces. These masks, which they call *ngontang,* represent a spirit returned from the world of the dead, beyond the sea, from the land of the whites. When the first whites arrived in Fang country, they were believed to be spirits of the dead returned to visit the living. According to Louis Perrois (1979:100–101), the interpretations of the meaning of these masks are as numerous as the explanations of the number of faces: "some see birth, life, sickness, death; while others: the father, mother, daughter; and still others: the four 'gods' of the Fang."

The *ngontang* may be used to seek out and destroy malevolent sorcerers (*nnem*) who use their powers to gain strength

and wealth. The mask may also dance at major family ceremonies including mourning, births, and important meetings. During the dance, the performer is possessed by a spirit (Perrois 1977:74, 92; 1979:101).

This mask once incorporated more than a dozen slender horn shapes projecting from the top of the head. The helmet was blackened with a hot knife, and the four faces were whitened with kaolin clay so that they would stand out clearly against the blackness of the nighttime forest. The delicate black patterns on each of the faces differ, but all include European-style mustaches, confirming Perrois's statement that the faces are intended to represent whites.

58. FANG, southern Cameroon, Rio Muni, northern Gabon / Head / Wood, metal tacks / H. 26.6 cm. (10½")

The reports of Günter Tessmann in the early 20th century described Fang reliquaries guarded by large heads. Tessmann suggested that the use of heads as reliquary guardians ante-dated the use of busts and full figures. Like the full-figure reliquary guardians, heads that have been used in this way are usually covered with a sticky varnish of palm oil, which is applied before sacrifices are offered to the reliquary. Many other heads, however, including the present example, lack this palm oil. Also, many of the heads are provided with holes or notches in the stalk or neck. These devices might have permitted the heads to be attached to a Fang harp—like

the famous example in the collection of Professor and Mrs. Mauricio Lasansky in Iowa City (Roy 1981 : 32). It seems quite possible that these objects were originally intended to deco-rate Fang harps, and were removed when the harps were damaged or at a time when few European collectors were interested in African musical instruments.

The sharp definition of the heart-shaped face and the hair-style, with its long vertical tresses at the ears, indicate that this head originated in the Ntoumou Fang area near the intersection of the borders of Rio Muni, Gabon, and southern Cameroon near the Ntem River.

59. TSOGO, Gabon / Reliquary guardian figure / Wood, metal / H. 33 cm. (13″)

The Tsogo (Tsogho, Mitsogho), occupy the high, cool forested mountains in the central area of Gabon, an area dissected by numerous tributaries of the Ogowe and the Ngounié Rivers. To the south live the Punu and to the north are the Fang. According to oral traditions, the Tsogo emigrated from an area of northeastern Gabon around the Ivindo River valley in the 13th and 14th centuries. Like other groups in Gabon, the Tsogo practice the cult of *bwiti*. One aspect of the *bwiti* religion is the cult of ancestors, *mombe*, in which reliquaries containing "human and animal bones, brass rings, grain, shells, coins, and jewelry . . . " are the focus of attention.

These reliquaries are guarded by wooden figures (*bumba*) like this one, which are buried in the relics up to the level of the abdomen (Perrois 1979:227; in Vogel 1981:196).

Tsogo figures and masks are characterized by a broad, vertical band of black paint or metal bisecting the forehead. The nose is always small, flat, and triangular, and the large, curving brows intersect the vertical band at the bridge of the nose. All published Tsogo reliquary guardians, including this example and the figure in the Tishman collection, and a third in the Royal Ontario Museum, are colored dark red with camwood powder.

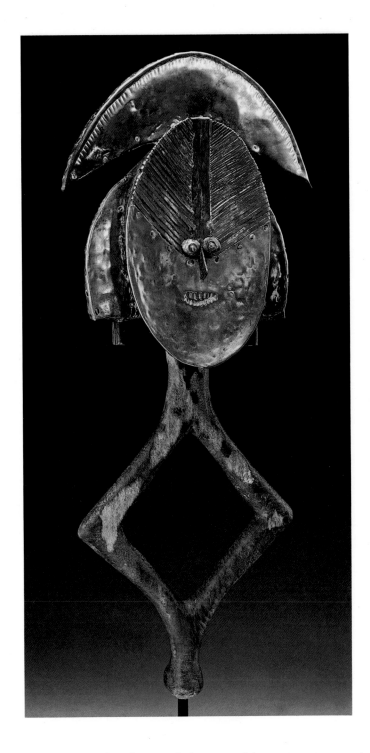

60. KOTA-OBAMBA, Gabon / Reliquary guardian figure, *mbulu* / Wood, brass / H. 61.3 cm. (24")

The most familiar of the Kota reliquary styles was produced by the southern Kota-Obamba. Like the Mahongwe *bwete*, the Obamba style figures were placed on a bag or basket which contained the long bones and skull of the founding ancestor of the clan. This was done to protect these relics from witch-craft and to help the living appeal to the ancestors for aid. Each of the reliquary baskets may have borne several figures: a larger figure representing the founder of the clan, and smaller figures representing founders of separate lineages. The head of the clan guarded the reliquary in his hut where sacrifices were made to it, invoking the health and well-being of the group, success in hunting, and human and agricultural fertility.

Combined with the relic containers, the Obamba figures were called *mbulu ngulu*, "image of the spirit of the dead," and are based on human forms. The oval, usually concave face is flanked by forms intended to represent the elaborate coiffures traditionally worn in the area. The metal that covers the figures was originally cut from brass and copper trade pots, but was later replaced by spools of wire and sheets of metal obtained in direct trade with Europeans.

61. KOTA-OBAMBA, Gabon / Reliquary guardian, *mbulu* / Wood, brass, copper / H. 43.2 cm. (17″)

Like the wooden figures from the Punu (catalogue no. 64), the Tsogho (catalogue no. 59) and the Fang (catalogue no. 56), this object and the two others by the Kota in the Stanley Collection were placed on woven bags or bark barrels that contained important ancestral relics. The figure protected these relics from the malevolent forces of witchcraft. According to Louis Perrois, "All the reliquaries in a village were grouped together under a small shelter away from the houses, in a sort of sanctuary for ancestors. In contrast to the Fang, whose Byeri cult became a family concern at the beginning of the twentieth century, the Kota—especially those in the south (Obamba, Mindumu, Mindassa, Bawumbu)—practiced a more communal cult in conjunction with initiation societies (*ngoye*) and on the village level (Perrois in Vogel 1981: 201).

This figure was produced by the southern Kota. It belongs to the "group 9", described by Alain Chaffin as a transitional style between the southern Shamaye and the northern Obamba styles. Chaffin has difficulty deciding, however, whether it is an Obamba style influenced by the Shamaye, a Shamaye substyle, or something else (Chaffin 1979: 276–7). Other objects in the group share the characteristic bulging forehead, downward-slanting almond eyes, outward flaring shapes below the ears, and a hairstyle that looks like a Napoleonic hat. Only one other object (no. 60, Rolin Gallery, N.Y.) shares the upwardly divergent lines on the brow that appear on this figure.

This same figure was once in the collection of George Gershwin.

EQUATORIAL FOREST: Ogowe River Basin

62. KOTA-MAHONGWE, Gabon / Reliquary guardian figure, *bwete* / Wood, brass, copper / H. 51.4 cm. (20")

Throughout Gabon, groups produce figures which serve essentially the same function—as reliquary guardians—but which are carved in quite distinctive styles (compare figures from the Fang, no. 56; the Tsogho, no. 59; the Punu, no. 64; and the Kota-Obamba, no. 61). The Kota, themselves, produce figures in two major regional styles. The northern Kota-Mahongwe produced figures called *bwete* in a concave leaf shape with a small, cylindrical crest projecting from the top of the head, and an oval opening in the lower stem that is oriented from side to side. The wooden figure is covered front and back with narrow strips of flattened copper and brass wire. The southern Kota-Obamba produced figures called *mbulu* with a concave, or less frequently, a convex face flanked by projecting shapes that represent hairstyles. These figures are covered with thin sheets of copper and brass on the front only. The lozenge-shaped opening in the lower stem is oriented in the same plane as the face (catalogue no. 60, 61).

Among the Fang (Fernandez 1975:740) and Kota (von Sydow 1932:48–51; Leiris and Delange 1968:327, University Museum, Philadelphia) and probably among the Tsogho and Punu as well, reliquary guardians began as full anthropomorphic figures with large cavities in the torso into which small bones and a single skull could be inserted. With the accumulation of larger quantities of relics, the figures' torsos were replaced by woven bags or bark barrels that contained the bones, and the full figures were replaced by heads among the Fang, and by very stylized shapes covered with metal and representing heads among the Kota. These were attached to the relic container, but could be removed and carried in dances.

This figure was formerly in the collection of Warner Muensterberger (Muensterberger 1955:no. 30) and is illustrated in Perrois's study of the arts of Gabon (Perrois 1979: no. 128).

63. VUVI, Gabon / Mask / Wood, kaolin clay / H. 38.1 cm. (15")

The Vuvi (Vouvi, Pouvi, Pubi, Pove) are grouped by George Murdock in the "Southern Cluster" of the "Northwestern Bantu" with the Tsogo, Lumbo, Aduma, and other groups in central Gabon. They live on either side of the Offoué River west and northwest of Koulamoutou. The Tsogo and Sango live to the south, the Ashira and Punu to the west, and the Aduma to the east. With all of these groups the Vuvi share the use of white, heart-shaped masks, which are used in mourning ceremonies to represent the spirits of deceased young women. In particular the Tsogo and Vuvi styles are characterized by high arching brows and a small, triangular nose—often blackened. Many Vuvi masks have two parallel "tear streaks" beneath the eyes, but lack the vertical black line that bisects the forehead on Tsogo masks and figures.

64. PUNU, Gabon / Female figure / Wood / H. 42.2 cm. (17″)

This beautiful figure of a woman was published in 1979 under the rubric "Ogowe River Style," because published information at that time did not make it clear which group in the region had carved objects in this style (Roy 1979a: 137). Since then, visitors to the collection who have studied in Gabon have stated emphatically that only the Punu (or BaPunu) have carved masks and figures with the distinctive oriental features we see in this figure and in the accompanying black and white masks. Other groups, especially the Ashira and Lumbo, have acquired objects in this style from the Punu.

Perrois (1979: no. 280) illustrates a similar figure, which he describes as a reliquary figure. It seems probable that this example was used, like Fang, Kota, and Tsogo figures, as a reliquary guardian. A figure in the same style, in the collection of the Musée de l'Homme, is still attached to a bag of relics (Leiris and Delange 1968: 238).

This object is also illustrated in Frans Olbrechts' important study of sculptural styles in Zaire, where it is attributed to the Punu (Olbrechts 1959: no. 11).

65. PUNU, Gabon / Mask / Wood / H. 29.8 cm. (12″)

In the drainage basin of the Ogowe River, the Punu, Ashira, and Lumbo peoples use masks whose distinctive style has often been compared to the *nō* masks of Japan. Most of these masks from the Equatorial Forests have white faces with brilliant red lips and often nine diamond-shaped scars on the forehead. The eyes are bulging half-moons. A number of different elaborate hairstyles are represented.

There have been many reports concerning the function of these masks. Hans Himmelheber (1960 : ill. p.309) indicated that the masks are worn by men who dance on stilts and carry a whip. They represent the spirit of a dead woman returned from the land of the dead. The Swedish missionary Efraim Andersson saw a similar mask in Zanaga village in the Kota area; there the mask was used in funeral ceremonies and in an ancestral cult (Andersson 1953 : 346). Several early reports state that the masks belong to a society called *mukui*.

Although the features are indeed accurate representations of the Punu ideals of female beauty (the horizontal lines between nostrils and ears represent small chains worn as jewelry in the area) white is the color of death.

66. PUNU, Gabon / Mask / Wood / H. 27.9 cm. (11")

While the white-faced masks produced by the peoples of the Ogowe basin appear frequently in collections outside of Africa, black masks in the same style are quite rare. Perrois suggests that the difference in color may indicate a change in function. Among the Galoa and the Ivili of the lower Ngounié River, white *okouyi* initiation masks are painted black to transform them temporarily into judgement masks with the power to discover witches (Perrois 1979:253).

Here, as in the white Punu mask in the Stanley Collection, the facial features are smooth, round, and naturalistic, with protuberant, crescent-shaped eyes; a large, domed forehead; delicate, slightly puckered lips; and a beautiful hairstyle.

67. KWELE, Gabon, Congo / Mask / Wood / H. 33.6 cm. (13″)

The Kwele traditionally have been a politically unorganized people who moved into the area between the Dja and Ivindo Rivers in the early nineteenth century. Kwele communities tended to fragment in the face of inter-lineage rivalries, and village elders countered this trend by diverting antagonisms through the rites of the cult of *beete*. Various magical materials, especially the flesh and intestinal contents of antelope, were combined into a stew, which was consumed by the entire village. The efficacy of the magical stew depended on the receptiveness of the villagers. To unite the community in harmonious interaction, a leader, in the form of a mask-being *kuk* (pl., *ekuk*) emerged from the forest and danced in the village, wearing seed-shell anklets. The *kuk* was followed first by singers and dancers who had escorted it from the forest,

and then by a line of all the villagers. A series of *ekuk* appeared in succession during the period that the *beete* medicine was being gathered and prepared. At the same time young men were initiated into the *beete* cult (Siroto 1972 : 58–63).

Most of the Kwele mask types are characterized by a two-dimensional, slightly concave, heart-shaped face, often painted white, and also by the addition of horns—downward-sweeping (as in this example), vertical antelope horns, or dramatic horizontal projections in the shape of a "W." They are a far-western extension of a heart-shaped-face tradition which stretches from the Gulf of Guinea to Lake Tanganyika. The flat, triangular nose, arching, pyroengraved eyebrows, and bulging, slit eyes are common to many styles in the basin of the Ogowe River, especially the Tsogho and the Fang.

68. NGBANDI (Angbandi, Mogwandi, Mbati), Zaire / Mask / Wood, European paint / H. 29.2 cm. (11")

The Ngbandi live between the Ubangi and the Zaire Rivers in northwest Zaire. The Ngbaka live to the west and the Azande to the east. The Ngbandi may have moved into the area they now occupy in the 19th century, displacing the groups they encountered, including the Binza, Mbudja, and Azande. Although they are primarily hunters and fishermen, during the colonial period when the Ngbandi area was an important source of rubber, they were forced to become rubber-collectors.

Published sources indicate only that masks were used in celebrations marking the end of initiation, *gaza*, for both boys and girls. "For about two months the young people are kept isolated in the forest, where they undergo traditional trials and initiations; the return to the village of the circumcised, or excised as is the case, is celebrated by three days of dancing" (Cornet 1972:322).

Information collected with the mask indicates that it was used in dances at about the end of World War I, before the arrival of an invading column of the Belgian *Force Publique*. The colonial army was defeated by the Ngbandi and fled, leaving behind pails of green and white camouflage paint. The mask was daubed with this paint and placed on an altar, never to dance again.

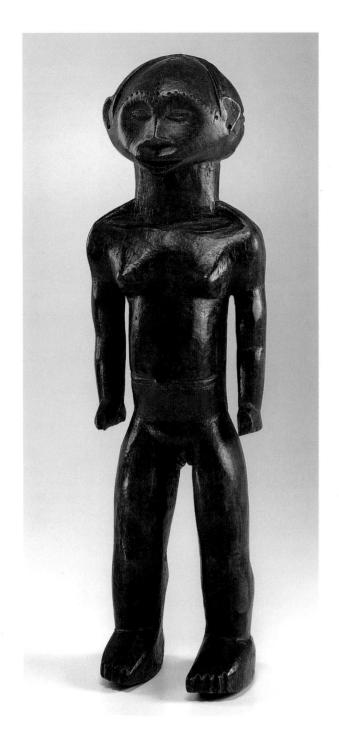
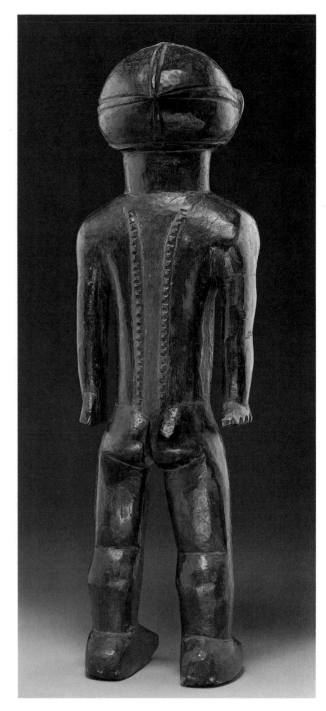

69. NGBAKA (Bwaka, Bouaka, Gbaya, M'Baka), Zaire / Female figure / Wood / H. 44.7 cm. (18″)

The Ngbaka live in northwest Zaire, on the plateau around Gemena, southeast of the Ubangi River. The Ngbandi live to the east. The Ngbaka appear to have been an intrusive nomadic group that moved gradually into the Gemena plateau area from the northwest and, as a homogeneous unit, only settled there in the 1920's. They are a politically non-centralized people who trace descent patrilineally.

Ngbaka figures are fully rounded with large, spherical heads. The face is often outlined in a distinctive heart shape. Like their Ngbandi neighbors, Ngbaka men and women wear a heavy ridge of scars that bisect the forehead vertically, and these are clearly depicted on both figures and masks. This figure is unusual for the care the artist has taken to represent ac-

curately the form of the collar bones and the musculature of the shoulders and arms. The hairstyle is cross-shaped, and there is a double row of chip-carved scars parallel to the spine.

Setu, the creator of the Ngbaka world, had a sister named Nabo. Following an act of incest between them, the Ngbaka people were created. The large, naturalistic figures carved by the Ngbaka represent Setu and his sister Nabo. The figures serve to protect the owner and his family from illness, miscarriage, bad harvests, unlucky hunts, and death. In the morning the figures are removed from the house and placed on an altar (*twabozo*). To cure illness a magical powder is sprinkled on the figure and on the patient, while at the same time prayers are offered to Setu to remove the affliction (*Brousse* 1958).

70. MANGBETU, Zaire / Pipe bowl / Wood / H. 14 cm. (5⅞″)

When the explorer George Schweinfurth visited the Mangbetu in 1874, he noted that the people were passionate smokers. He saw King Munza smoking a six-foot pipe in a very formal manner, assisted by a courtier whose only duty was to hold the pipe when the king was not inhaling. These pipes, and all of the court parapernalia Schweinfurth saw, were non-figurative. Indeed, no figurative sculpture was reported among the Mangbetu until well after the era of early explorers in the late nineteenth century (Kuennen-Jordan 1984).

Like the female figure in the Stanley Collection (catalogue no. 71), this beautiful little pipe bowl bears the marks of female beauty valued by the Mangbetu, including the elongated skull produced by binding the head in infancy with raffia bands. The length of the head is accentuated by the elaborate, flaring hairstyle, which is supported by thin, stiff, raffia strips that are inserted in the hairstyle as it is plaited. She bears long, dark lines like the ones painted on women's faces before important public appearances.

71. MANGBETU, Zaire / Female figure / Wood, metal, fiber / H. 43.8 cm. (17″)

The Mangbetu are a Central Sudanic people (Murdock 1959: 226) who speak a language called *Na Mangbetu* or *Kere*. Their major crops are bananas and yams. The Mangbetu migrated from the far north into the area they now occupy and, in about 1820, established their political hegemony in the area between the Bomokandi and the Uele Rivers. In 1870 George Schweinfurth visited King Munza in the Mangbetu capital called Nangazzi. Three years later Munza was defeated by the Azande (Kuennen-Jordan 1984).

A broad range of objects—including harps, pipe bowls, fig-

ures, stools, and storage boxes—were carved to reflect the power, wealth, and prestige of the Mangbetu nobility (Van Geluwe in Maesen 1967: 58). Wooden figures like this one apparently had no ritual significance (Cornet 1971: 296). They do, however, record accurately, Mangbetu traditions of dress and body decoration, as well as the distinctive elongation of the skull achieved by binding the soft cranial bones during infancy. Although absent from this object, Mangbetu figures often bear the same long, delicate tracings of dye that women apply to their bodies before important public spectacles.

72. MANGBETU, Zaire / Anthropomorphic pot / Fired clay / H. 27 cm. (10⅝")

The Mangbetu Kingdom dates from about 1820 when Na-biembali (the grandfather of the great King Munza who met Schweinfurth and other explorers) established political hegemony over many groups south of the Uele, including the Bangba, Makere, Mamvu and the Abarambo. By 1892 the Belgian colonial capital was established at Niangara, and taxes were being collected regularly from the male heads of households. The earliest descriptions of objects decorated with human figures or heads dates from 1891, when Casati described anthropomorphic harps and bark boxes among the Abarambo (Casati 1891 1:194). No early explorers described fired clay pots modelled in the shape of human heads until 1910, when Herbert Lang first collected such a pot in Niangara for the American Museum of Natural History. In 1911, the German Dr. Schubotz collected and illustrated two anthropomorphic pots, again near Niangara (Schubotz 1913:

ill. 13). Many similar pots were then collected between 1921 (British Museum) and 1928 (Cleveland Museum).

Two possible conclusions can be drawn: (1) that anthropomorphic art, including fired pots like this beautiful example, may have been made for the Mangbetu by their subjects, the Abarambo, and (2) that the pots were made by or for the Mangbetu to be sold to European visitors to Niangara to help accumulate the cash needed to pay Belgian taxes (Kuennen 1983).

The distinctive shape of the head was the result of cranial deformation. The flaring hairstyle that appears on many female figures is absent here. Because other pots with this style coiffure also have beards, these are assumed to represent men. The fact that it is very difficult to pour a liquid from most of these pots is additional evidence that they were non-functional, early tourist art.

73. ZANDE, Zaire / Figure / Wood, metal / H. 25.4 cm. (10")

Small wooden figures, ranging in style from extremely abstract human forms resembling large clothespins to fairly naturalistic anthropomorphic forms, are called *yanda* and are used by the *Mani* society, a commoner group which provided a balance of power against the ruling *Avongara* (or *Vurungura*) aristocracy (Burssens 1962). This female figure belongs to the type which is called *nazeze*, one of six figure types established by Burssens. The head of the society, called *Bandakpa*, gives the small figure magical powers by blowing smoke over it and smearing it with *libele*, a potion made of bark, plants and seeds. The figures are stored by the *Bandakpa* in a small hut near the society's meeting place.

The abbreviated, stump-like legs and underdeveloped arms are style characteristics which the Zande share with groups to the west, especially the Ngbaka and the Ngbande. However, the accumulation of ear and nose rings and the diamond-shaped face with its bulging eyes and dentate fringe are particularly Zande.

This object is illustrated in François Neyt's recent study of the sculpture of Zaire (Neyt 1981:69).

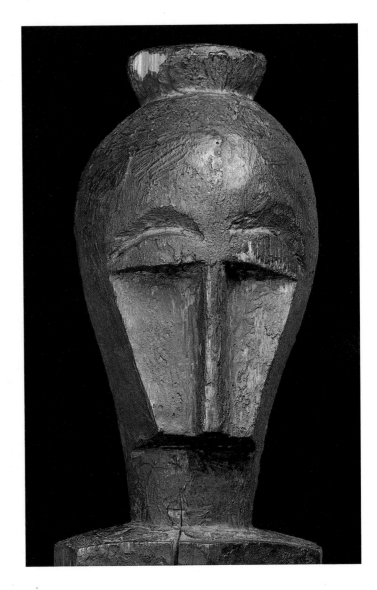

74. METOKO (Mituku), Zaire / Figure / Wood / H. 50.5 cm. (9½")

The Metoko are a forest people who live between the Lomami and Lualaba branches of the Zaire River between degrees 1 and 2 south of the equator. The Lengola live to the north and east, the Mbole to the west, and the Lega to the southeast beyond the Binja. Groups throughout this area share variations of the graded society called *bwami* by the Lega and *bukota* by the Metoko. As among the Lega, Metoko wooden sculpture is used within the context of the initiation society. The members of the two highest grades, *nkumi* and *kasimbi*, have exclusive control of some objects, while individual members of the other grades and members with special titles own some sculptures and other objects. "Similar to the Lega, all figurines have specific names, which refer to 'characters' (protagonists, models of certain types of behavior)." Within the context of *bukota*, figures are used in initiations, circumcisions, and funerals of members. They may also promote peace between feuding lineages (Biebuyck 1977: 52–53).

Both the Metoko and the neighboring Lengola sculpt figures with elongated, triangular faces bisected vertically by a long, straight nose. Arching brows form a distinctive heart shape. The body is so stylized that it may look like a haphazard arrangement of positive and negative geometric spaces, but it is possible here to discern the arms and the legs, knees touching.

75. MBOLE, Zaire / Mask / Wood / H. 48.6 cm. (19")

Very few examples of this type of object have ever been published. Daniel Biebuyck has written: "Little is known about this rare mask type, which is not mentioned in the earlier sources on the Mbole. It is possible the the mask was used in either the circumcision rituals or the lower level rites (*likomela*) of the *lilwa* association. In the *likomela* ceremonies young men and some young women, guided by a ritual expert, pass through a series of trials and learn basic social and ethical concepts. They are allowed to see and touch some of the ritual objects used at the higher levels of the *lilwa*" (Biebuyck 1984).

There are certain unaccountable stylistic similarities with masks used far to the west, in Gabon and the Congo. The round, flat masks of the Tseye Teke are quite similar in composition, and some white masks of the Tsogho and other groups near the Ogowe use a similar treatment of the eyes, eyebrows, and especially the nose.

It seems quite unlikely that such a mask was intended to be worn over the face, for it is quite flat on the back and there are no holes for eyes.

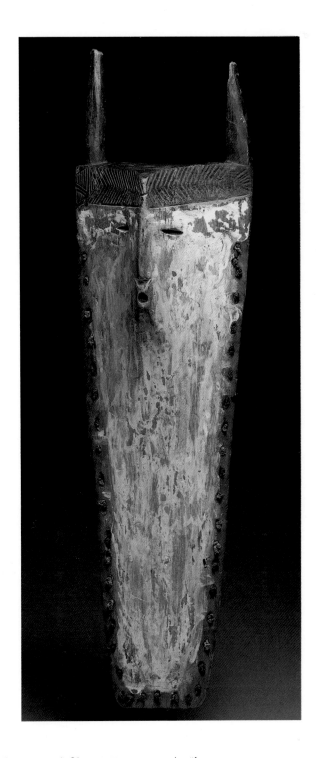

76. LEGA, Zaire / Mask, *kayamba* / Wood, fiber / H. 55.9 cm. (22")

The Lega live in eastern Zaire, just west of the northern end
of Lake Tanganyika. The Bembe, Bangubangu and Boyo live to
the south, and a number of small groups, including the Ba-
bemo, Bila, Kwame, and Kanu live to the north. The Lega do
not have a system of chiefs or other hereditary rulers. Instead,
political organization is provided by the *bwami* society, which
has several grades. All men aspire to work their way upward
from the lowest grade, through a series of initiations, to the
two highest grades, *yananio* and *kindi*. Very few ever reach
the highest *kindi* level. The goal of membership in *bwami* is
moral perfection, taught or symbolized by proverbs, dances,
and objects.

This mask may be of the rare type called *kayamba*, used in
the *yananio* rites (cf. Biebuyck 1973:plate 37). "The catego-
ries of *kayamba*, large, horned, whitened wooden masks . . .
are extremely rare. *Kayamba* masks are kept in collectively

held baskets . . . " (Biebuyck 1973:164,183). "The rare,
horned *kayamba* mask with whitened face has a very narrow
range of meaning. It represents a clever and shrewd person:
'*Kayamba*, who comes from afar, cannot be bad.' When used
in pairs . . . however, *kayamba* masks may portray a confron-
tation of Kabimbi, the Clever-One, and Kalulungula, the Liar"
(Biebuyck 1973:214).

This mask is certainly unusual, even for the Lega. The incised patterns between the bases of the horns are not characteristic, and the back is unusually and perfectly flat, with no
eye-holes. Unlike the *kayamba* masks illustrated by Professor Biebuyck, the facial features on this mask are all restricted
to a small area high on the face, a design which creates an
enormous chin from which once hung a raffia beard, now
nearly gone.

77. LEGA, Zaire / Mask, *lukwakongo* / Wood / H. 26.9 cm. (10½″)

All Lega art is used by members of the *bwami* society, an age-grade hierarchical association of initiates which comprises five grades for men (*kongabulumbu, kansilembo, ngandu, yananio, kindi*) and three complementary grades for women. The men's grades are subdivided into various initiatory cycles. Theoretically, all grades are open to all men and women in Lega society, although in actuality 95% of men reach the rank of *kongabulumbu* but most never reach the second highest grade, *yananio*. The difficulty of advancing in *bwami* is expressed by the Lega aphorism: "Those who suffer from dizziness do not get to the top of the tree; they turn back at the intersection of the branches." Wooden masks are owned primarily by the members of the second highest grade (*lutumbo lwa yananio*), although the highest, *kindi*, grade shares rights of ownership. Masks of this type, called *lukwakongo*, are used in several ways in *yananio*. "They are worn on the face

or attached to the forehead so that the beard covers the face; they are sometimes fastened to the temple, to the back of the head, to a knee or an arm; they are placed in a row or in a circle on the ground or piled up together; they are attached to a fence or to the central pole of the initiation hut; they are carried in the hand or swung around or dragged over the ground; they are held under the chin and so on" (Biebuyck 1973: plate 62). Masks are links to the dead and as such are symbols of the continuity of *bwami*. The Lega refer to the mask as "the limb that remains of the dead one."

Although most Lega masks are formally simple, this example, with its small, round eyes and mouth and its slender, long nose, surrounded by the heart-shaped outline of its face, is unusually severe. J. W. Mestach is studying a group of at least five masks with these characteristics that all appear to be the work of a small Lega workshop (Mestach 1984).

78. LEGA, Zaire / Mask, *lukwakongo* / Wood, kaolin / H. 19.3 cm. (7⅝")

"Classified as *lukwakongo*, this mask type is owned in most Lega areas by individual male members of the second highest grade (*yananio*) in the *bwami* association. This mask appears in several phases of the *yananio* initiations and is used in different ways: carried in the hand, held under the chin, dragged by its beard over the ground, fixed to a palisade and sometimes to its owner's hat. In most rites all participant *yananio* display and use their own masks so that the masks always occur as a group. The precise meanings vary widely depending on the actual contexts of usage. The emphasis may be on the mask as a whole, or on specific parts (such as the beard, as the symbol of the elders; or the open eyes without pupils representing the character 'Who-does-not-see-well')" (Biebuyck 1984).

79. LEGA, Zaire / Figure, *iginga* / Ivory, beads / H. 12.5 cm. (4¹⁵⁄₁₆″)

"Classified like other anthropomorphic figurines under the generic term *iginga*, the figurine is owned by male members of the highest grade (*kindi*) in the Lega *bwami* association. The objects are insignia of rank, and initiation devices that express the positive and negative aspects of the value code of the *bwami* association. Because of the attachment of beads, this particular figurine may represent the character Kakinga (young maiden). This and other ivory figurines used in several phases of the *kindi* initiations are displayed in configurations or danced with by their owners" (Biebuyck 1984).

80. LEGA, Zaire / Figure, *iginga* / Ivory / H. 10.5 cm. (4")

Both this figure and the smaller, lighter colored figure (catalogue no. 79) were used by the highest *kindi* grade of the *bwami* society. The contrast in forms is quite typical of Lega art which includes a broad range of independent, nonconformist sculptural styles that are difficult to characterize. These figures ". . . illustrate formulations of virtue and nonvirtue as defined by *bwami*. Each of the ivory or bone figurines has an aphorism of its own; each has a concrete and restricted meaning. Only rarely do particular usage, mode of presentation, and context add something to the meaning" (Biebuyck 1973:218).

This female figure, with its carefully carved necklace and scarification patterns on head and abdomen, resembles quite closely a figure that Biebuyck acquired in 1952, called Keitula, "the heart of the one who holds the wickerwork rattles" (Biebuyck 1973:plate 84).

81. BEMBE (eastern), Zaire / Mask, for the *alunga* association / Wood, fiber, pigment / H. 49 cm. (19")

Masks of this type are used by the men's *alunga* association of the Bembe, who live on the western shore of Lake Tanganyika. The two-faced mask was carved in two sections, bound together back-to-back, and was worn over the head as a helmet with a large crest of feathers projecting dramatically from the top.

"The mask, called *ibulu lya 'alunga* (head of *'alunga*), represents a powerful spirit of the bush (*m'ma mwitu*). Traditionally preserved in a secret cave (*lwala*), the mask is brought to a shack (*lutanda*) built in the bush outside the village for the secret initiation of new members into the *alunga* association, for hunting cult gatherings, for social control functions, and for public dance performances. It is worn by a specialist who ranks highest in the association and who holds the title of 'spirit of the bush.' This expert knows not only how to wear the cumbersome mask but also the specialized dances, and he is versed in a manner of speaking and singing in a hoarse gutteral voice. Whenever the mask is donned, it is topped with a crown (*ehala*) of quills and feathers; a rigid fiber collaret is attached to the bottom holes of the mask. Specialized dressers (*ba'wa icwalelo*) help the expert dancer put on the mask and the large fiber costume (*asamba*) with genet hides and straps of bark" (Biebuyck 1972 and 1984).

Janiform masks and figures seem to be particularly popular among the Bembe (cf. Roy 1979a:no. 138, Bembe figure). With its four huge concave orbits and star-shaped eyes, and its total lack of other facial features, this mask is a particularly clear reminder that African art is representative, not representational.

SOUTHERN SAVANNAH

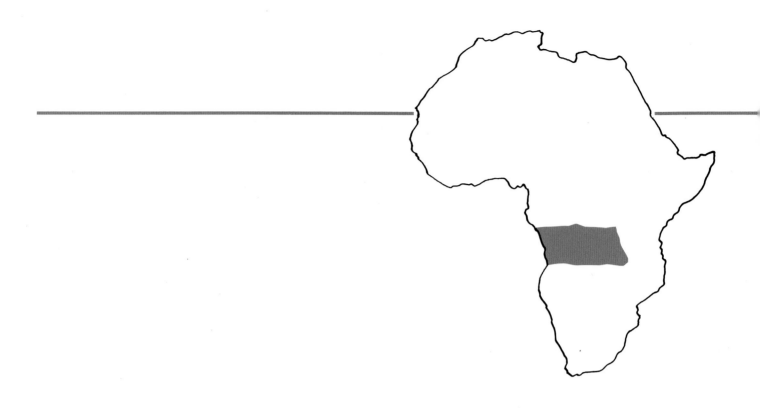

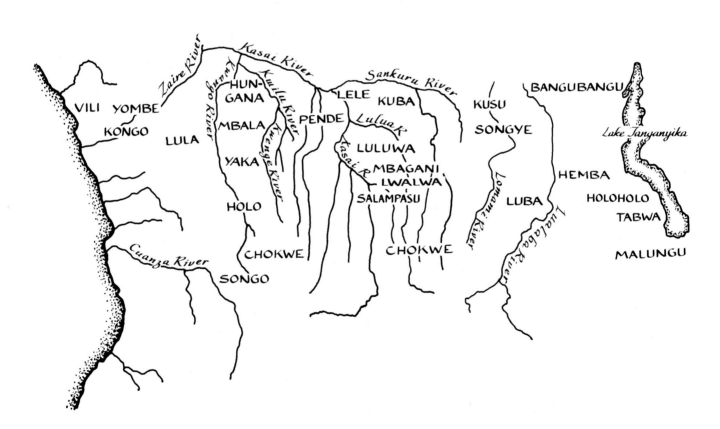

The Southern Savannah Style Area

The Southern Savannah style area corresponds to the broad band of open savannah grasslands that stretches across Africa south of the equator from the mouth of the Zaire River in the west to Lake Tanganyika in the east. To the north lies the thick tropical rain forest of equatorial Africa. Broad bands of heavy forest follow the valleys of the Kwango, Kwilu, and Kasai Rivers far to the south into Angola. In the west, groups such as the Kongo, Vili, and the Bembe may inhabit areas that are heavily forested, but the sculpture they produce is related to styles across the savannah. The great tributaries of the Zaire River are the major geographical features in the area, and as in the Equatorial Forest, these rivers seem to have served as highways for the movement of cultural traditions. Groups such as the Yaka are more closely related stylistically to the Teke, far downstream, than they are to groups a short distance to the west, such as the Kongo.

Emerging from their long passage southward across the forest, Bantu-speakers adopted American crops such as maize, peanuts, tobacco, and sweet potatoes, after 1500, as well as Malaysian crops including yams, bananas, and coconuts.

Both geographically and politically the Southern Savannah is strikingly similar to the savannah grasslands of the Western Sudan. Large-scale, centralized political states were established by the Kongo in the west, the Kuba in central, and the Luba in southeastern Zaire, and by the Lunda and Chokwe in northern and eastern Angola. The Portuguese first visited the Kingdom of the Kongo near the mouth of the Zaire River in 1482, and they maintained considerable influence for about a century. In 1507 the king and many of his subjects were converted to Christianity, and as a result, much Kongo art includes Christian imagery.

Most of the groups in the Southern Savannah produce magical figures called *nkisi* that are given supernatural power by the addition of potions to horns or other containers on the head, back, or abdomen. The original sculptural forms are transformed as the objects accumulate power and are activated by numerous clients. The presence of many great kingdoms in the savannah has led to the creation of a rich court art, including flywhisks, scepters, prestige containers, finely woven cloth, and royal portraits. Their fine workmanship and valuable materials attest to the rank of the owner. Many of the savannah groups, especially in the Kwango/Kwilu Rivers area, use masks to celebrate the initiation of young men into adult village society.

It is possible to distinguish at least five major substyles in the Southern Savannah. At the mouth of the Zaire River, groups that formed the Kingdom of the Kongo produced a naturalistic style in which the modelling of the face and musculature was carefully rendered, and great attention was paid to details of personal adornment. In the Kwango/Kwilu Rivers area, figures typically hold the hands beneath the chin, legs flexed, the lower body shapes forming rhythmic parallel planes. Red, white, and black pigments are often used in geometric patterns. In the Kwango/Cuanza area, the eyes are surrounded by deeply sunken orbits, and the double arch of the brows joins over the bridge of the nose. The art of the Kasai/Sankuru Rivers area is often decorated with fine patterns based on woven designs. Masks, figures, and anthropomorphic pipe-bowls and containers depict the very distinctive hairline, sharply angled at the temples. Masks are often decorated with an accumulation of shells, beads, and cloth that reflects the wealth of the royal family. Finally, in the area east of the Sankuru River, sculpture shares large, fully rounded forms, massive heads with high brows, elaborate hairstyles, and rich, dark surfaces enhanced by the raised textures of complex scarification patterns.

82. VILI, People's Republic of the Congo / Side-blown trumpet, *kithenda* / Ivory, metal / L. 44.4 cm. (17½")

The Vili occupy an area just north of Cabinda along the Atlantic coast in the Congo (Brazzaville). They belong to a group of peoples, including the Yombe, Sundi, and the Kongo themselves, who speak the KiKongo language, and formed the ancient Kingdom of the Kongo, encountered by the Portuguese in 1482 when they arrived at the mouth of the Zaire River. The capital of the kingdom, Mbanza Kongo, in what is now Angola, was known by the Portuguese as San Salvador. The most famous of the Kongo kings was Afonso I, who began his rule in 1506 and became the first Christian king, beginning an era of great European influence on the religion and culture of the area.

Political leaders in the region of the mouth of the Zaire River used court regalia similar in type to the leadership objects used in other great West African states. Canes, staves, flywhisks, hats, and trumpets (like this example) marked an individual as a ruler. A manuscript published in 1665 by an Italian priest includes a drawing of Queen Gonga of Matamba with her attendants. Visible in the long procession behind her are heralds playing side-blown trumpets to announce the arrival of the queen. These trumpets were also sounded at assemblies of chiefs, to announce alliances or war, and at the marriages and funerals of important people. François Neyt, who illustrates this piece (1981:87–89), notes that it reproduces the scene of the triumphal entry of a Vili queen. The royal figure is seated cross-legged on a leopard skin. The tiny finial represents the royal elephant, a symbol of power and political rule.

Close inspection of the figure's chest and a radiograph (Neyt 1981:fig. V.7) reveal metal eyes and two large areas where metal objects have been inserted into cavities in the ivory carving. Neyt suggests that the largest of these objects may be a tiny metal figurine.

The two bands of carving on the lower area of the horn represent bands of cowrie shells. The beautiful orange-red surface is the result of repeated applications of palm oil and centuries of extensive handling.

SOUTHERN SAVANNAH: *Lower Zaire River Area*

83. KONGO, Zaire / Funerary figure, *phemba* / Wood / H. 52 cm. (20½")

One of the important style characteristics of the Lower Zaire River area is the tendency toward naturalism, especially in funeral portraits like this one, which were placed on the grave of the deceased to help the spirit on its way to the afterlife. The life-like carving of the sensuous lips, fully-rounded cheeks, and beautifully modelled chin, and the great care given to the details of scarification on the back and upper arm, and to the chief's hat, *mpu*, contribute to our feeling of sadness as this mother offers her child on bent knees. Raoul Lehuard has suggested that the child may be dead, and that these figures represent the wife of the chief presenting to her husband their first child, still-born or dead soon after birth. In such a case, the theme is certainly not that of perpetuation of the royal family (Lehuard 1977).

Similar figures, representing both men and women in common poses and engaged in daily tasks, were produced in stone, extremely light wood, and more recently in cement. The Stanley Collection includes a similar wooden figure produced by the Sundi (Roy 1979a: 157).

84. KONGO, Zaire / Magical figure, *nkisi* / Wood, feathers, glass, metal, animal teeth, shell, cloth / H. 29.2 cm. (11½")

Ethnic groups throughout the Southern Savannah style area are linked by the common use of objects like this one. These objects are given magical curative or destructive powers by the addition of effective materials (*bilongo*) to the abdomen, back, top of the head or elsewhere by a ritual specialist, *nganga*. These materials may be placed in a horn that projects from the top of the head (catalogue no. 93), in a rolled snakeskin belt or necklace (catalogue no. 111), or in a cylindrical resin *kundu* gland that projects from the abdomen and is sealed with a "mirror of mystic vision, indicating the ritual expert's power to see beyond the glassy surface of the river, or the sea

[beneath which the underworld lies]—to penetrate the secrets of the dead" (Thompson in Vogel 1981:210).

Such objects may act as positive or negative forces on behalf of the client, protecting his family from diseases and spells and from witches and thieves, or, on the other hand, bringing confusion and death to his enemies.

This figure, which has accumulated a crown of feathers, metal anklets and collars, and a number of leopard teeth and shells, holds a medicinal plant to its mouth. The *nganga* may chew this plant to produce a viscous green sap that he spews over his clients as part of the healing ritual.

85. KONGO (Muserongo), Zaire / Magical figure, *nkisi nkonde* / Wood, iron nails, glass, resin / H. 51.4 cm. (20")

Certainly the most dramatic of the magical figures produced across the Southern Savannah are the *nkisi nkonde* (plural *minkinsi minkonde*) figures that are usually called "nail fetishes" in the popular literature on African art. Most frequently, these consist of anthropomorphic figures with one arm raised and holding a weapon (often missing). Usually these figures are balanced on their toes and leaning forward aggressively, ready to strike. As in this example, large numbers of nails, tacks, pins, arrow heads, and metal blades of all shapes and sizes protrude from the torso and limbs—so many that, in some cases, only the head and feet emerge from a prickly mass of pointed iron.

These magical figures are given a specific power when an *nganga*, a ritual specialist or pharmacist who acts on behalf of his client, applies medicinal/magical ingredients. The powers of the *nkisi nkonde* may be positive or negative: they may act as agents of healing, justice, revenge, and oath-taking. To seal a contract, bind an oath, or finalize a treaty, the parties involved may drive blades part-way into the figure and then wrap them with raffia twine to bind the agreement. Individuals may activate the magical power of the figure by driving a nail or tack into the surface, thereby stirring the figure to action. "A specialized blade, with flaring head and tapered stem, 'looks like a *baaku*,' an ancient kind of Kongo knife. A *baaku* was a specialized instrument used to extract the 'milk' of the palm wine tree. This blade, when inserted in *minkondi*, was believed to have the power to kill by supernatural means, by analogy with the term, *baaka*, the latter meaning not only 'extracting palm wine' but also 'demolishing, destroying.' It is a kind of blade which classically functions within the *minkisi* range of metaphoric medicines of 'attack'" (Thompson 1978:216–7). The great numbers of blades and points driven into the figure are witness to the numbers of clients who have sought the aid of its magical powers.

This figure, formerly in the Paris collection of Max Itzikovitz, was acquired in the Ambrizette area of Lower Zaire at the end of the nineteenth century. It is illustrated in Raoul Lehuard's study of *nkisi* figures (Lehuard 1980:123, no. 69).

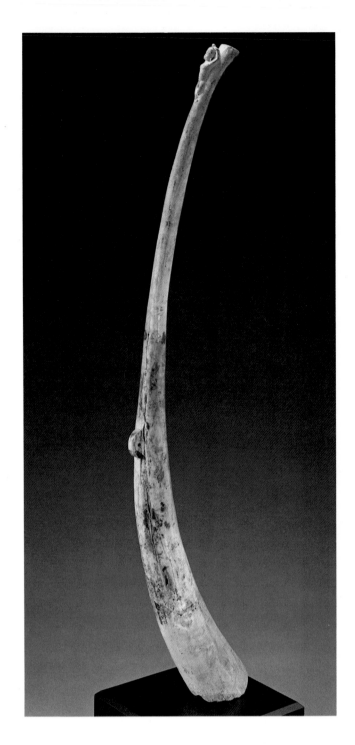

86. KONGO, Zaire / Trumpet / Ivory / H. 110 cm. (43½″)

This large musical instrument was owned by a sixteenth-century notable (*mfumu*) of the Kingdom of the Kongo, in whose tomb it was discovered. Like the Vili trumpet (catalogue no. 82) it marked its owner as a person of prestige and political power.

The trumpet has been carved from a very large ivory tusk, and the artist removed much of the material to lighten it and to provide the central protruding ring for support. The finial is decorated with the small but very lively figure of a dancing girl with her arms raised above her head and her legs crossed. Such animated poses are rare in African sculpture, although they occur more frequently in Kongo art. Like most ivory trumpets from the area, the widest part of the mouth (bell) had been wrapped in hide, but because it had deteriorated severely, the hide was removed.

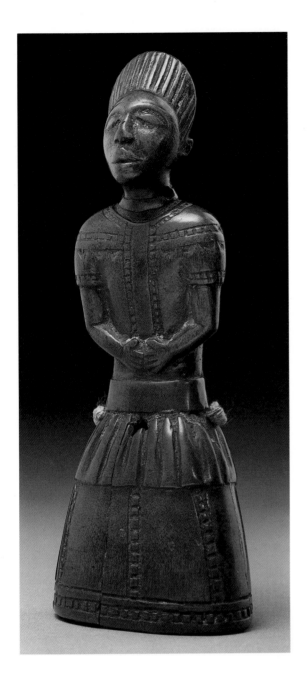

87. YOMBE (Mayombe, Bayombe, Majombe), Zaire / Bell / Wood / H. 14.5 cm. (5¾")

This object represents the figure of a woman from the lower Zaire River area; she wears an embroidered jacket and a full, flaring skirt in the Portuguese style of the sixteenth century. The skirt is pleated at the waist, bound by a broad waistband, and spreads below to form the mouth of a bell. Three small pieces of wood suspended on a cord serve as clappers. A hole pierced through the figure's neck permitted the bell to be worn as a pendant necklace. Joseph Cornet indicates that generally such bells were called *madibu* and were symbols of the diviner or *nganga*, who called upon the *nkisi* spirits during ceremonies by ringing the bell. More specific information has been provided for this piece by the family that owned it; they stated that it was worn by the *phemba*, or senior woman of the clan.

88. YAKA, Zaire / Figure, *biteki* / Wood / H. 49 cm. (19")

While both Yaka and Suku style characteristics are present in this figure, Arthur Bourgeois has attributed it to the Yaka in his new book, *Art of the Yaka and Suku* (Bourgeois 1984a). He writes: "In my book [the figure] is published as Yaka principally because the nose-mouth-chin combination is foreign to the repertoire of Suku statuette variations as I know them, combined with the fact that the expanded lower torso does not have the distinct horizontal ridge, which is generally the case when Suku statuettes otherwise adopt [the Yaka] upturned-nose and other expressive features. On the Suku side, I admit the eyes, headpiece, and breasts can be seen on prominent Suku examples. But the clincher for me is a statuette I had carved in the Yaka village of Pasanganga, west of Popokabaka, whose torso, legs, and chin are rather like your piece, minus the breasts. I am not suggesting that your piece is recent, however [it was collected in the 1880's], but that this neck-torso, shoulder-arms, and leg treatment can be found among either the Yaka or the Suku.

"The size of this carving among both the Yaka and Suku is distinctive of lineage *biteki* used as a charm to contain and control evil influences of a curse and its hereditary effect. Yet at the same time it can be used to protect property and inflict injuries on witches or other malefactors. The female gender here does not help in determining the precise type of lineage *biteki* but my guess is *Nkosi*, the most widespread variety among the Yaka and their neighbors. Attachments were undoubtedly suspended from the arms and/or a bag enclosing charm-medicines accompanied this figure originally.

"The carved personage is shown with a headpiece that denotes authority depicted in a reflective attitude, yet personifies the 'influence' that has resulted in past misfortune, sickness, and death, as well as the threat of these in the immediate future. In this sense it is associated with the power of elders although it is not an 'ancestor figure.'"

89. LULA, Zaire / Mask / Wood, fiber, blue and white pigment / H. 43 cm. (17″)

There are still some questions about the ethnic origin of this unusual mask. It was originally identified as Holo, but recently two scholars familiar with the Kwango/Kwilu area have stated emphatically that it could not be Holo (Bourgeois and Maesen 1984). Although the mask bears some resemblance to the face of the Holo "queen" illustrated in François Neyt's recent study of the Holo (Neyt 1982 : ill. 33 and Neyt 1981: fig. VI 13), it does not resemble Holo masks illustrated in the same publications. Arthur Bourgeois has written that it is quite similar to a mask in the Donald B. Ross collection in Indianapolis: "The bulging, flattened eyes relate this image to Yaka statuettes from the Kabama area in proximity to the Lula . . . The surrounding plaque-like extension with a separate headpiece attached in back relates to Nkanu masks. The

forehead shape, however, does not relate closely to Lula statuettes . . . The elongated, narrow nose coming nearly to a point is closer to Zombo masks collected around the turn of the century near Kibokolo . . . Holes beneath the eyes, mouth, and ears are very unusual" (Bourgeois 1984b).

The Lula live just west of the Kwango River, between the Dikidiki and Ntandu to the west and the Yaka to the east. The influence of Yaka sculptural forms is very evident in this mask, and indeed, the Lula state that their clans came from the Yaka area (Boone 1973 : 139−40). Bourgeois feels that the function of the object may have been similar to *kakungu* among the Yaka: "To prevent witches, the *baloki*, from entering the [initiation] camp and causing harm to the initiates . . . " (Bourgeois 1980 : 43).

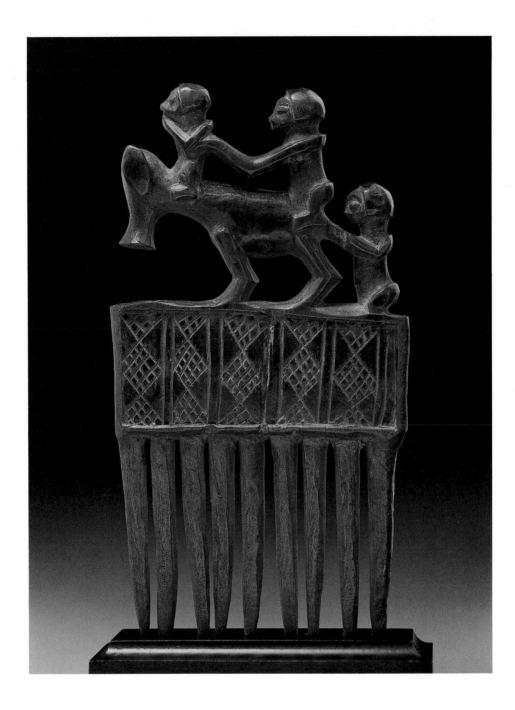

90. HOLO, Zaire and Angola / Comb, *pendu* / H. 14.9 cm. (5¾")

The Holo live on both sides of the Kwango River, on the border between Zaire and Angola; the Guillaume waterfall marks the northern limit of their country. Forming a cultural transition between the Yaka and Suku peoples to the north, and the Chokwe and Chokwe-related peoples (especially the Imbangala and the Songo) to the south, the Holo share style characteristics of both areas.

This comb bears a group of three human figures and an animal—an ox or a donkey. The largest figure sits astride the hindquarters of the animal and supports a smaller figure, perhaps an infant, on the beast's neck. A third large figure trails behind, grasping the animal's tail. In the seventeenth century Portuguese Capuchin monks established St. Mary of Matamba mission in the Holo capital, and since then Christian symbols have greatly influenced Holo sculpture. "In the

course of time the Holo picked up elements borrowed from Christianity and integrated them in a quite individual, syncretic manner, into the *nzambi*-cult" (Neyt 1982 : 44). It does not seem inconceivable, therefore, that the figure group on this comb represents the Holy Family on the flight into Egypt.

On the other hand, many Songo and Holo carvings represent European traders and explorers riding on oxen. Such traders travelled extensively through the bush in the eighteenth century carrying beads, cloth, brass tacks, and other articles which were exchanged for slaves, ivory, and rubber. Oxen were preferred over horses, because their large hooves did not sink into the soft sandy soil, and because oxen are more resistant to trypanosomiasis (sleeping sickness) than horses (Bastin 1982b : 23–4).

91. MBALA or KWESE, Zaire / Mortar with human figure / Wood / H. 42.2 cm. (17")

The Mbala and the Kwese live in close proximity within the territory of Gungu (Bambala-Bakwese, Lutshima-Ndjari, and Mulikalunga Sectors) between the Kwenge and Lutshima Rivers. To the west live the Yaka and Suku, and to the east live the Pende. Throughout the area the emphasis on a heart-shaped face is quite common.

The object was employed as a mortar for grinding tobacco into snuff, or perhaps for grinding the ritual kaolin used in the installation ceremonies of a regional chief. The elaborate carving of the regal figure, with its prestigious hairstyle and beard, indicates clearly that the object was not designed to be used by just anyone (Bourgeois 1984b).

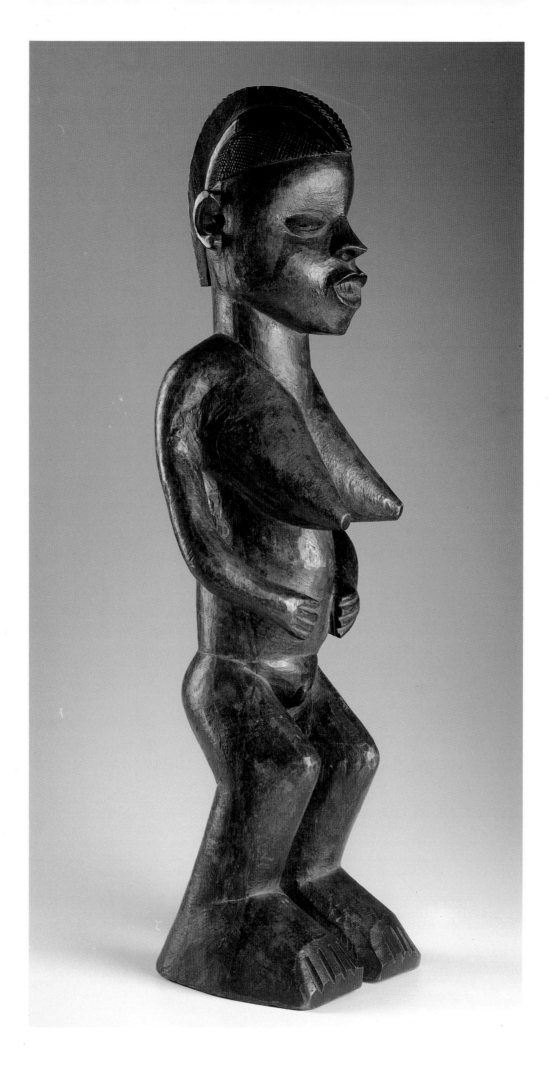

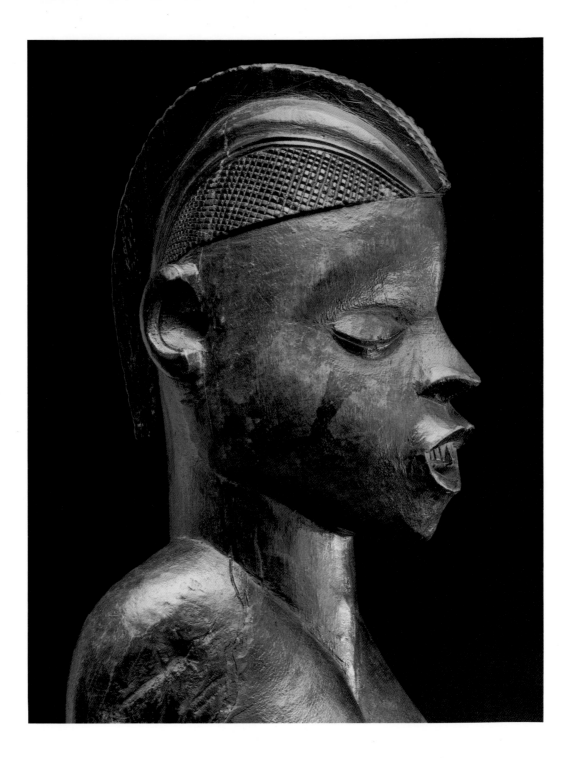

92. MBALA (Pende?), Zaire / Female figure / Wood / H. 48.2 cm. (19")

Experts have failed to agree about the ethnic identity of this beautiful figure of a woman. It has been known as Pende since it was collected in the 1920's, although we do not know if this identification is based on field data. Malutshi Mudiji-Selenge, the Zaire National Museum expert on the Pende, has stated emphatically that the figure is Mbala, rather than Pende. "She is certainly Mbala, because she bears stylistic traits that are undeniably associated with that tribe, notably the treatment of the hairstyle with three longitudinal bands of hair, of which the central one is larger than the others, the open mouth with some teeth unfiled, large and jutting breasts . . . If the figure was carved by a Pende, he must have been truly 'Mbala-ised.' It is known that certain Pende from the left bank of the Kwilu were subjected to some Mbala influence by way of the Kwese [who live between them], but they never went so far as to use

the treatment of the hairstyle we see here, which belongs to the Mbala, and especially the Suku" (Mudiji-Selenge 1984). Nevertheless, Professor Albert Maesen, former head of the ethnology section at the Royal Museum for Central Africa, has called it Pende, as have others. It is certain that the figure combines style characteristics of both groups, evidence of the cultural interchanges between the peoples of the region.

Much Mbala sculpture is used in the investiture of chiefs, and certainly such a large and regal figure must have represented a female ancestor. "In Mbala society, where descent is matrilineal, maternity figures are not simply the symbol of the chief's authority, but are an essential element of the cult of ancestors; she incarnates in a way the female founder of the lineage; this is why she is carefully guarded in the chief's house" (Cornet 1972:92).

93. PENDE (eastern or Kasai), Zaire / Magical figure, *nzinda* / Wood, shell, horn, cloth, beads / H. 102.3 cm. (40")

Like other groups across the Southern Savannah from the Atlantic to the Great Lakes, the Pende produced magical figures that were given power by the addition of materials prescribed by a diviner/healer called *ngongo*. This figure, in the style of the Kasai Pende, is of the same style, and may be by the same hand as five other figures of the same type in American and European collections. The best known in this country is in the collection of the American Museum of Natural History and was illustrated in *African Art in American Collections* (Robbins 1966:206). Other examples are in the Musée Royal de l'Afrique Centrale, near Brussels, and in a Chicago private collection. A fourth figure, illustrated by Margaret Trowell (1979:397) and William Fagg (1964:52) when it was in the collection of the Musée de la Vie Indigène in Kinshasa, is now lost. Finally, the sole example for which there is field documentation is illustrated in Father de Sousbergh's study of Pende art (1958:150–151, ill. 273), and is now in the collection of the Jesuit Fathers in Louvain. The figure was

collected by Father J. Delaere before 1929 in a village close to the mission of Muhaku (Gungi chiefdom). De Sousbergh says that it was called *nzinda* and was a "powerful magical fetish" used in divination. Heavy cords were attached to both arms to permit it to deliver oracles: "in the darkness of its hut, it would lean either to the left or to the right." It could transform the bullets of the white colonial forces into water, and it would indicate the number of warriors the village should send into battle against the whites by making marks in the sand with the horn attached to the top of its head.

All these pieces share the long, triangular nose and the protuberant, almost conical eyes. The arms are bound with heavy cords; a turtle shell hangs suspended at the waist. A heavy horn projects from the top of the head, and all are colored red. Until recently, since the 1930's, the figure in the Stanley Collection had been kept wrapped in an attic in Belgium. As a result, its bright red pigment has been preserved.

94. PENDE (eastern or Kasai), Zaire / Mask / Wood, metal tacks, fiber / H. 23 cm. (10")

The Pende live between the Kasai River in the east and the Kwilu River in the west. They immigrated into the area they now inhabit from the Atlantic coast of Angola at the end of the eighteenth century. They are politically non-centralized, the chiefdom made up of a group of clans. The primary function of the chief is religious. He is a link with the ancestors who provide human and agricultural fertility.

There are two major Pende styles. The western, or Kwilu Pende are best known for their distinctive *mbuya* masks, each characteristically marked with a high, domed forehead, downturned mouth, heavily lidded eyes that appear either very sad or drugged, and a continuous, unbroken eyebrow line across the forehead. The eastern Pende live on the west bank of the Kasai River, north and downstream of Tshikapa. Their style is far more geometric and colorful than their neighbors' to the west. Masks are decorated with systems of red and black triangles on an earth-red background, and the eyes are often narrow, bulging slits.

This small, delicate mask was collected near Tshikapa among the Akwa Pinda clan. It is of the type used in *Muniya'angi* dances that are prescribed by the diviner (*ngongo*) "in case of contagious disease or repeated abortions" (Neyt 1981:146). A very similar mask, perhaps by the same artist, is illustrated by Father de Sousbergh (1958:68,ill. 73), from the collection of a Madame Schwob. A third, named *kiova*, was collected by Professor Albert Maesen in 1954 in Luaiya village, also part of the Akwa Pinda clan. Professor Maesen's notes indicate that the mask performed to restore equilibrium in the village when there had been much sickness (illustrated in de Sousbergh 1958:ill. 72; Maesen 1984). Father de Sousbergh notes that such masks, smaller than a human face, can be seen by women and are worn by the followers and the family of the chief.

95. HUNGANA (Hungaan, BaWana, Wana), Zaire / Magical figure / Wood, red pigment / H. 58.5 cm. (23")

The Hungana are a small group that occupies the west bank of the Kwilu River in Zaire. The Pende live to the southeast, and the Mbala are their immediate neighbors to the west. They are closely related culturally to the Mbala, and their sculptural forms have been heavily influenced by Mbala art. The Hungana are best known as smiths, and in fact the root of their name *hunga* means forge. They live in widely dispersed settlements, often comprising the minority of larger Yaka, Suku, and Mbala villages.

The Hungana style is distinguishable by the striking hairstyle that was once worn in the region, consisting of three long, parallel plaits of hair extending from the brows far down the back. In addition, the style is characterized by a thin, cylindrical neck that rises from a large, swelling torso. The head projects far forward. Like the figures carved by other groups in the area, especially the Teke, Yaka, and Suku, the arms are bent at the elbows and the hands touch the chin. The best-known examples of these large wooden figures are in the University Museum, University of Pennsylvania (Fagg 1970: 79) and the Museum für Völkerkunde, Berlin (Krieger 1965: no. 267, ill. 224). All three share the hairstyle and hands-to-chin pose. A number of smaller figures in the same style are suspended like a belt around the Berlin piece. This, an acquisition note stating that the object was a "fetish from the Sankuru," and comparison with the function of objects by neighboring groups seem to indicate that the figures were magical, rather than ancestral.

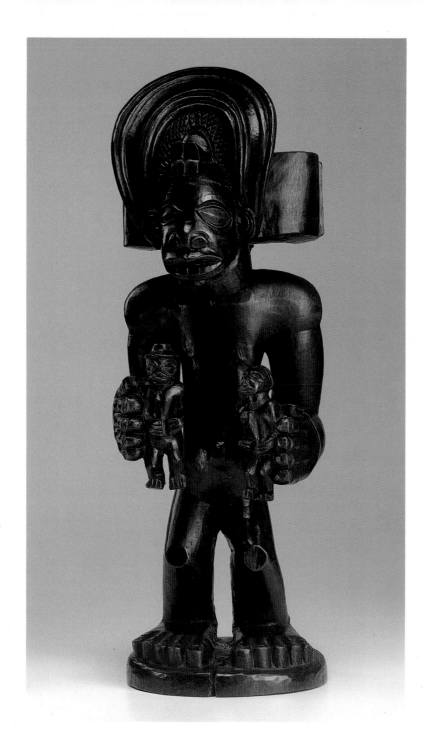

96. CHOKWE, Angola / Figure of a chief, *mwanangana* / Wood / H. 37 cm. (14")

This is the figure of a Chokwe chief wearing the elaborate crown called *cipenya mutwe*. He holds the small figures of male and female ancestors, *mahamba*, in his hands. The figure stands with knees slightly flexed, upper body inclined forward. Much care has been given to represent accurately such anatomical details as the joints and nails of the hands and feet, and the musculature of the shoulders, arms, and back.

The figure was carved in the first half of the nineteenth century in the Chokwe homeland near the sources of the Kasai and Kwango Rivers. It was collected by José de Andrade Toscano in about 1895. Toscano was on a punitive expedition led by Captain Artur de Paiva against King Dunduma of Bie's

village of Ecuvongo. The village was destroyed in order to avenge the death (in about 1890 or 1891) of one Silva Porto, a death for which King Dunduma was held responsible. Ecuvongo village was located in the area between the Cuquenna and Chishonga Rivers in the western Moxico region where many of the greatest figures of the Chokwe "homeland style" were carved. Until recently, this figure had been in the possession of José de Andrade Toscano's Portuguese descendants.

The only other chief figure holding *mahamba* protective ancestor figures known to exist, is in the collection of the Museu de Etnologia in Lisbon (Bastin 1982a: ill. 105). That figure, one of a male/female pair, is stylistically very close to the figure in the Stanley Collection. The Lisbon figure wears

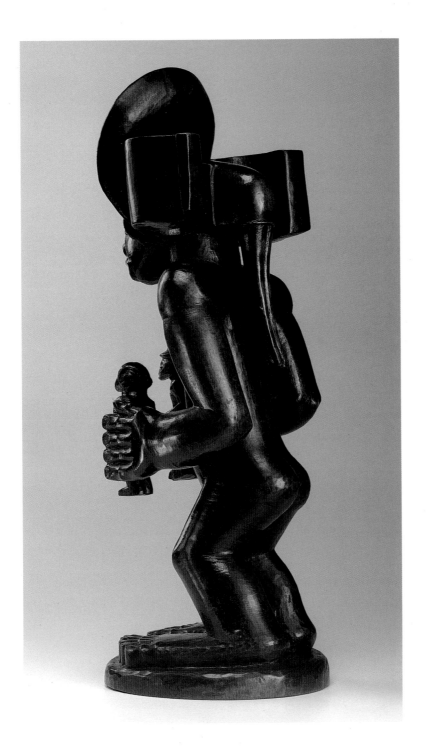

a different crown, called *mutwe wa Kayanda*, but because the details of the hands and feet, the musculature of the back, and the reserve coloring of the wood to produce decorative bands of light natural color against a dark background are common to both, one is led to the conclusion that both figures are the work of one artist or one workshop (Bastin 1984b). In subject matter, pose, attention to detail, and brilliance of carving this piece can best be compared to the figures of the culture-hero Tshibinda Ilunga in the collection of the Museu de Antropologia da Universidade in Porto (Bastin 1982a : ill. 81 and cover) and in the collection of the Kimbell Art Museum in Fort Worth (Bastin 1982a : ill. 85).

The small figures held in the chief's hands represent an-cestor spirits that serve as intermediaries between the creator spirit and mankind. These *mahamba* protect the chief and his family and village against *wanga*, the evil forces enemies activate through sorcery and the use of occult powers. "The majority of the *mahamba* protect hunters and assist child-birth: to obtain game and to give birth are the essential obligations of men and women, in order to maintain the sustenance and secure the continuity of the group" (Bastin 1982a : 54).

The chief figure in the Stanley Collection is also illustrated in the catalogue of the June 29, 1983 auction at Christie's in London, number 184.

97. CHOKWE, Angola and southern Zaire / Mask, *mwana pwo* / Wood, copper tacks, fiber, conus shell / H. 25.5 cm. (10")

The feminine mask *mwana pwo* and its male counterpart, *chihongo*, are noble masks, worn together by men in dances which magically bring fertility and prosperity to the village. The male mask represents the spirit of power and wealth, while the female recalls the ancestress. The *pwo* performer is dressed like a woman, and he dances elegantly and gracefully, showing the women of the village the value of graciousness and good manners (Bastin 1984a : 212–13).

Marie-Louise Bastin has attributed this *pwo* to the "Expansion Style," Kwilu/Kasai substyle, from the region of Xasenge near the right bank of the Kwango. She notes that two additional masks by the same hand in the collection of the Museu de Etnologia, Lisbon (AB 255 and AB 256), are illustrated in her recent publication, *La Sculpture tshokwe* (Bastin 1982a: fig. 42,43). These were produced by an artist working in the first thirty years of this century.

The scarification patterns on the face include the cross-shaped *chingelyengelye* on the forehead and the solar disk joined by "tears," *masoji a mitelumuna nyi cijingo.*

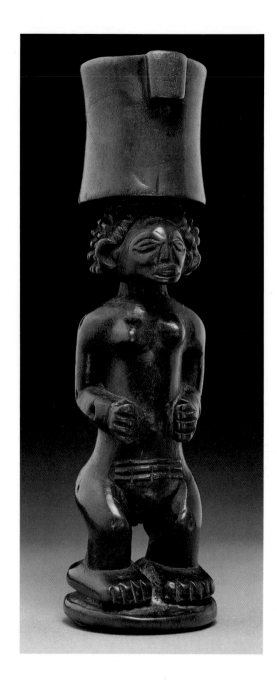

98. CHOKWE, Angola and Zaire / Snuff mortar, *tesa ya makanya* / Wood / H. 14.3 cm. (6″)

Marie-Louise Bastin writes: "This anthropomorphic snuff mortar must have belonged to an important person. I would classify it in the expansion style, sub-style of the Kwilu-Kasai. The *mikonda* scars, in parallel, horizontal lines, decorate the pubis. During adolescence these are applied to all women, who without such marks would never find husbands. These scars in relief have an erotic function. They are caressed by the husband during sexual relations with the intention of having many descendants" (Bastin 1984b).

The object was once provided with a tiny wooden pestle attached by a short cord. Then, together, the mortar and pestle could be used to grind tobacco leaves into a fine powder.

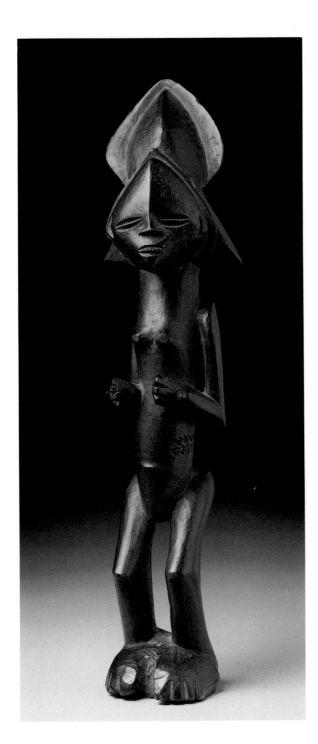

99. SONGO, Angola / Female figure / Wood / H. 26.1 cm. (10″)

The Songo belong to the "Lunda Cluster" of George Murdock's Central Bantu (Murdock 1959:293). They are closely related to the Chokwe, Luchazi, Luvale, and Ndembu. As among the Chokwe and the Lwena, Songo ruling families are of Lunda origin. Numerous trade routes cross Songo country, and through their trade in beeswax and ivory, the Songo came in contact with most of the groups in the upper basin of the Kwango River. While many of the traits of the Songo style are traceable to contact with the Chokwe, the distinctive shape of the shoulders of this figure can best be compared to the shoulders of the larger Yaka figure (catalogue no. 88).

This small, delicate female figure wears a flame-shaped cap that may mark her as a member of a ruling family. A hole, pierced through from one side of the cap to the other, permitted the figure to be worn suspended around the neck. Marie-Louise Bastin indicates that the figure may represent an ancestor. It belongs to a small corpus of carvings by a single artist working at the end of the nineteenth century, including a snuff mortar in the Sociedade de Geografia, Lisbon, another snuff mortar formerly in the Bandeira collection in Portugal, and a decorated scepter in the Museum voor Land en Völkenkunde, Rotterdam (Bastin 1984b).

100. KUBA, Zaire / Female figure / Wood / H. 57.8 cm. (23″)

Experts on the art of the area have attributed this figure to the northern Kuba of the Sankuru River area, and, more specifically, to the Shoowa. The hairstyle is certainly quite typical of the "Kuba" groups in the confluence area of the Kasai and Sankuru Rivers. Emil Torday describes the hairdressing of the ruling hierarchy of the Kuba: "The men shave the whole head, keeping on the top of the skull only a small tuft of hair just large enough to be hidden by the headdress; the temples and forehead are carefully shaved, but the line of implantation of the hair can nevertheless be distinguished and this line is indicated on the dolls and on the carvings . . ." (Torday 1910: 49,169).

The Kuba tradition of carving "portraits" of *Nyim*, or kings, has been very well documented by Jan Vansina, Joseph Cornet, and others. Far less is known about female figures, however. Vansina indicates that "the large statues used in the late nineteenth century by the central Kuba were mainly female figures employed during the boys' initiation . . ." (Vansina 1978: 212).

101. KUBA (Ngeende), Zaire / Mask, *bwoom* / Wood / L. 48.3 cm. (19")

The Kuba kingdom is made up of several small ethnic groups—
including the Pyaang, Bulaang, Kaam, and the Ngeende—
organized around a dominant group, the Bushoong, and ruled
from a centralized court at the capital at Mushenge (Nsheeng).
These groups, all claiming common origin and direct descent
from the first man/founding ancestor, Woot, together number
about 200,000. The greatest of the Kuba kings was Shyaam
aMbul a Ngoong, who reigned from about 1600–1620, and is
the great culture-hero of the Kuba. He is credited with the
introduction of manioc, palm oil, tobacco, raffia-weaving, and
embroidery.

Masks appear at the initiation of young men, and recreate
the myths of the foundation of the Kuba kingdom. One of the
three major characters represented by masks is *bwoom*, por-
trayed with a large, bulging forehead, enormous nose, and
other coarse features. "According to certain legends, *bwoom*
is simply the representation of the appearance of a [nature]
spirit *ngesh* as it was seen one day by the initiates of the
nkaan [initiation group]" (Cornet 1982:264). François Neyt
has attributed this mask to the Ngeende (Neyt 1981:163, ill.
VIII.10), who live just east of the core Bushoong.

102. LELE (Leele, Bashilele), Zaire / Pipe / Wood, brass tacks / L. 31.7 cm. (12½″)

The Lele, or Bashilele, live south of the confluence of the Kasai and Sankuru Rivers, just west of the Kuba kingdom. To the south and west live the Wongo.

There has been a free interchange of cultural characteristics with the Bushoong in the Kuba heartland, and it is often quite difficult to distinguish between the Lele and Bushoong styles. Both groups use, and represent in their sculpture, the same elaborate hairstyles, with the hairline shaved to a triangle above the ear. Both groups use a similar repertoire of patterns to decorate masks, figures, bowls, cups, and pipes like this extraordinary example.

The Lele often decorate utilitarian objects with human faces, whose features are more frequently reduced to geometric stylizations than they are among the Bushoong. Here, typically, the mouth is a simple "D", the nose is severely conical, and the eyes are keeled lozenges with concave, almond-shaped orbits. The cheeks are broad and flat, and the chin is quite round. The hairstyle sweeps elegantly back to form a pair of curving ram's horns.

The stem of the pipe is carved of wood, and includes the *ibol* weevil emblem, indicating that the object was made for the royal family. The flaring end is decorated with carved antelope horns. The original bone mouthpiece is missing.

103. LULUWA (Bena Luluwa, etc.), Zaire / Mask / Wood, fiber / H. 37.2 cm. (15″)

This mask was collected in the Luluwa village of Tshene Ditu near the southern Kete area. François Neyt has written that "various traits of this object . . . are reminiscent of Kete culture: the rounded forehead and the convex, triangular face" (Neyt 1981:191,196, ill. IX.8). The high, domed forehead and enormous sunken orbits of the eyes are very similar to the smaller Luluwa mask in the Stanley Collection (catalogue no. 105). Finally, the similarities with the Mbagani mask (catalogue no. 109) are striking.

104. LULUWA (Bena Luluwa, Bena Moyo, Bashilange, Baluba ba Mwaanza), Zaire / Snuff mortar / Wood / H. 12.8 cm. (5")

The Luluwa comprise a large number of peoples, all of whom inhabit the region south of the Kuba and the Kete between the Kasai and the Sankuru Rivers. The Luluwa River flows through their lands—hence their name, "people of the Luluwa." To the south live the Mbagani, Lwalwa, Southern Kete, and the Salampasu. The Luluwa were ruled by a *kalamba* chief who acted as a judge. Because of Luba incursions which have forced the Luluwa south into contact with their many neighbors, there has been an active interchange of cultural characteristics with the Kuba, Pende, Chokwe, and Songye. Sculptural influences of each of these groups are visible in Luluwa figures. The most obvious Luluwa style trait is the use of elaborate scarification patterns, especially on the face, neck, and abdomen.

Like other groups in the region, including the Chokwe (compare catalogue no. 98), the Luluwa carved small mortars for grinding tobacco into snuff. Here the top of the head has been hollowed out and supplied with a tiny lid. The distinctive squatting pose, with elbows resting on the knees and chin resting in the hands, occurs frequently among the Luluwa and very rarely elsewhere in Africa. The emaciated condition of the figure, with its ribs showing through the flesh, the enlarged head, and stupefied expression may reflect the effects of hemp smoking, introduced by the first great chief, *Kalamba* Mukenge, to substitute for the use of palm wine (Van Geluwe in Maesen 1967 : 40).

SOUTHERN SAVANNAH: Kasai/Sankuru Rivers Basin

105. LULUWA, Zaire / Mask / Wood / H. 24.2 cm. (9½")

While Luluwa figures covered with elaborate scarification marks are numerous, the masks produced by these people are rather rare. The best known is the example published by Professor Maesen in *Umbangu* (1969:28), which shares with this example the black and white patterns of scars against the natural color of the wood, and dark, concave orbits around narrow eyes. There are, at the museum in Tervuren, five additional masks of the same style, four from the collection of the Compagnie du Kasai. It is apparent that these masks consti-

tuted a type that may have been created by a single workshop, for they represent the work of at least three different artists.

Information about the function of these masks is very sparse, but both Huguette Van Geluwe (in Maesen 1967:40) and Joseph Cornet (1971) agree that they were used in circumcision rites.

This mask is remarkable for its small size, the delicacy of the facial features, especially the thin nose and everted mouth, and for the thinness and lightness of the carving.

106. LULUWA, Zaire / Magical female figure / Wood / H. 22 cm. (11″)

The Luluwa are famous for their figures of women with elaborate raised scarification patterns on the neck, abdomen, face and limbs. These are used by the *tshibola* cult, a group of women who have lost several children in succession—either by abortion, at birth, or in infancy. Such women consult a diviner who may attribute the problem to the presence of an ancestral spirit called *tshibola*. The woman is initiated, has a figure carved like this example, and performs rituals intended to facilitate the reincarnation of a family ancestor into her lineage group. This is important, because an ancestral spirit's rebirth in her next child will ensure its survival into adulthood. The woman's magic figure is carried in a wrapper at her belt, where she later will carry her newborn child.

The female figures are depicted complete with the elaborate scars, hairstyles, and jewelry that conform to the Luluwa ideals of adult female beauty, and that will attract the *tshibola* spirit to the figure. The figures are covered with red powder mixed with oil (*tukula*) or with chalk. One of the most noticeable characteristics of the Luluwa style is the emphasized umbilicus (commonly herniated in black Africa), which is the link between the mother and the child (Timmermans 1966: 19–23, Bastin 1984a: 219).

The face of this figure should be compared with the Luluwa mask (catalogue no. 105) which bears similar painted patterns, the same heart-shaped depression around the eyes, and the same line of the jaw and chin.

107. SALAMPASU, Zaire / Mask / Wood, copper, vegetable fiber / H. 35 cm. (14″)

The Salampasu, who live south of the Lwalwa and the Mbagani and west of the Lulua River, once had a reputation as fierce warriors and headhunters. They continue to be skilled hunters. During the warrior society's admission ceremonies, the initiate was painted red, and performed a dance called *matambu*. Masks of three different types, made of different materials but stylistically quite similar, were used in the initiation of young men (Bogaerts 1950:401−2). Photographs taken by Michel Huet of male initiation rites in the Luiza region show fiber, wooden, and copper-covered masks—all performing together. The three types represent the three ranks of male society: the hunters, warriors, and chiefs (Paudrat in Huet 1978:194).

Both types of wooden masks as well as the knotted fiber masks have large, bulging foreheads overhanging short, triangular noses and small, deeply recessed eyes. The mouths are always open, showing needle-sharp teeth. The fiber coiffure consists of balls of stiff interwoven fiber strands.

108. LWALWA (Lwalu), Zaire / Mask / Wood / H. 29.5 cm. (11½″)

Four types of Lwalwa masks are used in the ceremonies of the *Ngongo*, a society responsible for the initiation and circumcision of young men. Both male *nkaki* masks and female *cifola* masks are worn by men in dances intended to pacify the spirits of the human victims which were required for entrance into *Ngongo* (Van Geluwe in Fry 1978:83). Each performer commissions the mask type that he prefers from the carver, who often is also the village chief and the organizer of these mask dances (Timmermans 1967:83).

This male *nkaki* mask is of the type called *mvondo*. It was held steady on the wearer's face by a cord that passed through the hole beneath the nose and was clamped between the teeth.

A very similar male *mvondo* type is illustrated in the catalogue of the Tishman collection (Vogel 1981:230): The mouth of the Tishman piece is less rectangular and the eyes lack the frames that are present here, however. There is also another rather more rudimentary example in the J. P. Barbier collection (Fagg 1980:133). The present example is illustrated in Neyt's study of Zairean sculpture (1981:206). It is remarkable for the care given to the geometric patterns in the coiffure, for the elegant definition of the face—especially the nose, scars, and mouth—and for the very fine, smooth surface.

109. MBAGANI (Binji, BaBindji), Zaire / Mask / Wood / H. 34.9 cm. (14")

The Mbagani live south of the Luluwa, west of the southern Kete, north of the Lwalwa, and east of the most northerly Chokwe, between the Kasai and Luluwa Rivers. The Mbagani should not be confused with the Binji who live just east of the Kuba, south of the Sankuru River, and who have been heavily influenced by Kuba culture. Both the names BaBindji and Mbagani are pejoratives, the former given by the Luba, who considered them under-dressed savages, and the latter given by the Lwalwa, who found their language difficult to understand (Boone 1961:179).

The sculpture of the Mbagani, and especially this mask, has been heavily influenced by the Luluwa and the Lwalwa. The sunken orbits of the eyes, protruding and elongated chin, and high forehead are quite similar to the forms of the Luluwa mask (catalogue no. 103). The elongation on a vertical axis, with a long, straight nose, and the support by a cord passed through the hole beneath the nose are quite similar to the Lwalwa mask (catalogue no. 108). The major, distinguishing Mbagani characteristic is the use of white pigment in the large area around the eyes (compare with Mbagani mask in Cornet 1972:159, coll. Jef Vander Straete).

Cornet states that such masks "accompanied circumcision and certain ceremonies of initiatory societies" (1972:166).

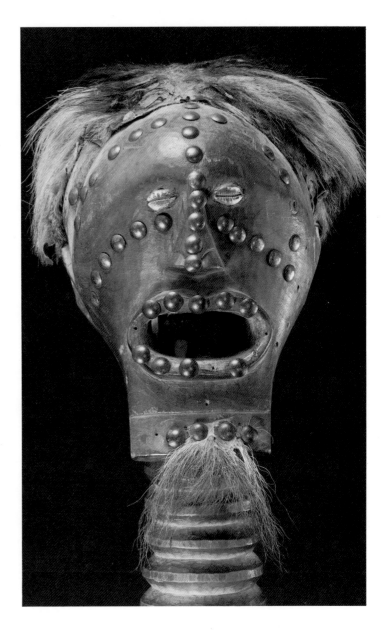

110. SONGYE, Zaire / Magical figure / Wood, monkey fur, brass tacks / H. 48.9 cm. (19")

Like the other Songye figures in the Stanley Collection, this object was once given magical power through the application of potent materials, probably in a series of snakeskin collars bound around the annular decorations on the neck. Other potions were probably also stuffed into the large cavity of the rather ferocious and frightening mouth.

The head is covered with the hide and fur of a monkey,

giving the figure its name—*Ya Nkima,* "the monkey." But the most unusual feature of the object is the long, ringed neck, which may represent the distinctive scarification patterns that were once popular in the region. Such neck scars were worn especially by the Tetela, who live near the Kalebwe sub-group of the Songye who produced the object, and by the Lu-luwa, whose sculpture bears similar patterns (Mestach 1984).

III. SONGYE (Bekalebwe), Zaire / Magical figure / Wood, horn, metal tacks, snake skin / H. 89.5 cm. (39")

Most of the ethnic groups that occupy the Southern Savannah style region, from the Kongo on the Atlantic coast to the Bembe and Tabwa on the shores of Lake Tanganyika, produce magical figures, often called *nkisi* (or "fetishes" in the art literature) which are given magical power in the form of accumulated materials applied by the herbalist/magician/healer called *nganga*. The forms of these objects are usually dynamic, the poses aggressive and even threatening; the functions can be malevolent or benevolent, depending on the particular prescription that the *nganga* uses. The Songye produce the most numerous and distinctive of these magical figures.

J. W. Mestach has studied the Songye in depth, and has provided the following notes: "The large collective community figures [including this very large example], considered most often to be benevolent, were kept hidden from view. Other malevolent figures were kept outside the village. Only priestesses were permitted to use the objects in special cults, principally during nights of full-moon. The statues were carried by means of thick leather cords which were passed through the rectangular openings beneath the arms. The benevolent statues were considered to be, among other functions, the protectors of the villages and of children who sometimes bore the name of the statue (most frequently *Ya Ntambwe* 'lion,' or *Ya Nkima* 'monkey').

"These same large Songye statues could often be found among the regalia of the Kuba king. There, too, they were used as objects of high magic and great power, the Songye having the reputation among the Bushong [Kuba] as masters of sorcery and fetishism" (Mestach 1984).

112. SONGYE, Zaire / Magical figure, *nkishi* / Wood, hide, raffia / H. 43.2 cm. (17″)

While much of the sculpture produced by the Songye is expressive, this figure, and others by the same artist in collections in Europe and the United States, is remarkable for its malevolent grin, enormous hooded eyes, and arching brows. In contrast to most African figures that are frontal and symmetrical, this *nkishi* turns its head sharply to the left, confronting its next victim.

J. W. Mestach has written: "This is the type of figure (of the *nkishi* category) that belonged to the entire community, and that had the top of the head charged with magical materials (*bajimba*) and surmounted by a horn. Similarly the facial cavities were stuffed with magic. Magically charged, it must have been a male figure.

"The statue personifies a terrible and malevolent 'spirit,' and that is why its head is turned, for this expresses hidden

intentions, lies, among the Songye. The same representation is found among the Luba of Kasongo Niembo and represents the spirit *Umba Kilubi*, Prince of Darkness, whose kingdom *Kalunga ka Musono* is located in the bowels of the earth. In the underworld, he is the ferryman on the river of death, invoked by the sorcerer who calls upon the spirits of the dead.

"The Stanley Collection figure comes from a workshop in the *Bena-Kibeshi/Belande* area, but statues of the same style are found among the Nsapo [tribe] in the Kananga area, a group that originated from the Beneki (Songye sub-group), who have occupied the Kabinda territory for over a century. The hairstyle is reminiscent of the hairstyle of the Luba Shankadi, who are neighbors" (Mestach 1984).

113. SONGYE (Batempa), Zaire / Magical figure, *nkishi* / Wood, copper tacks and twisted rings / H. 17.8 cm. (7″)

In contrast to the very large *nkishi* figures that watched over an entire community, this small figure protected a family or an individual against sorcery, malevolent spirits, and diseases. In this case, the proliferation of tacks driven into the figure indicates that it protected against smallpox (Mestach 1984).

"The form indicates that it comes from the Batempa (a Songye sub-group) towards the Pania-Mutombo sector" (Mestach 1984).

This tiny figure, covered with enormous tacks, and with a rather sad expression on its face, recalls the suffering of the Biblical character Job.

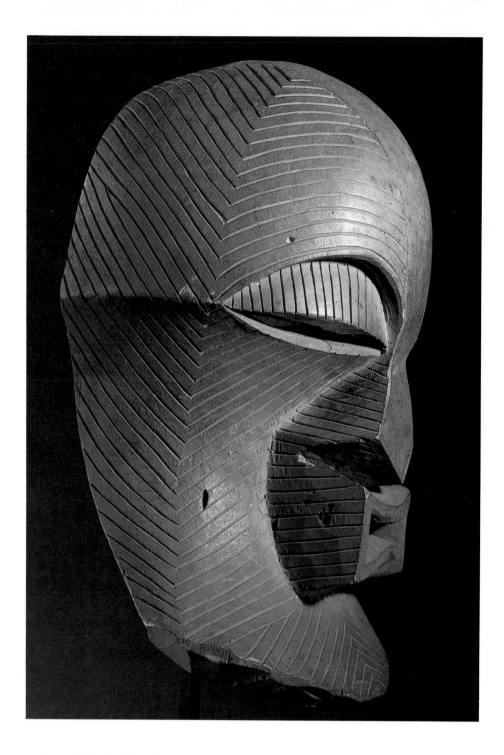

114. SONGYE/LUBA, Zaire / Mask / Wood / H. 40.6 cm. (16")

The German folklorist Leo Frobenius, who visited south-eastern Zaire in 1906–7, provided the earliest description of the use and function of Songye masks based on observations of their traditional context. His notes (published by Ernst Vatter 1926: 107,108,181) indicate that, at that early date, the masks were associated with a cult of the dead and were used in the prevention and curing of illness, and perhaps also in the expulsion of the spirits of the dead.

In the past, masks in this style have been attributed solely to the Songye, and are referred to as *kifwebe*, "wooden mask" (Merriam 1978). It became clear that there were problems with this attribution when Joseph Cornet published several similar masks as Luba in the catalogue of the Bronson collection (Cornet 1978: 276–9). In fact, it appears that both the

Songye and the Luba produce these masks, especially in the area of transition between the two groups. This mask was collected in the village of Kahombo, in the Songye-Bekalebwe area of Kabongo. J. W. Mestach has found two figures wearing masks with some of the same style characteristics, one of which was collected in the Bena Mwo chiefdom, near the Bena Lumba, in this same Kabongo region.

The mask is unusual in that it lacks holes around the rim for attaching a costume. Of the seven masks by the same hand studied by Mestach, two lack holes, indicating perhaps that these are magical or "fetish" masks to which sacrifices were made but which were not worn. The two holes in the cheeks seem to confirm this, for some magical figures have similar holes for attaching monkey hair (Mestach 1984).

115. SONGYE (Nsapo), Zaire / Cup / Wood / H. 15 cm. (6")

"The [very worn, smooth, and soft] patina of this cup indicates that it must have been used as a cult container for palm
oil, rather than as a cup for drinking palm wine, the more
usual function of cups from the area.

"The foot motif that forms the base is a symbol of power
and of the taking of territory, and also appears on certain objects from the Luba, Songye, Kuba, and Shilele. The same
motif sometimes decorates objects used by the sculptor and

the smith. The chiefly beard connects this cup with the ancestral cult, and its linear form recalls the style of the Luluwa, as do the wave-like scars and the concentric circles on
the forehead. The mouth, however, is typically Songye.

"Like the Nsapo-style neckrest (catalogue no. 116), I would
group this cup with a large number of Songye objects that
show a mixture of styles of different origins" (Mestach 1984).

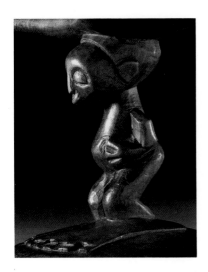

116.
SONGYE (Nsapo-Beniki), Zaire /
Neckrest (pillow) /
Wood / H. 13.6 cm. (6″)

Neckrests of this type are quite common in East and Central Africa. They permit the user to sleep on one side, with his arm and shoulder against the floor, and his head supported at a comfortable height. Joseph Maes has devoted a study to the neckrest collection of the Tervuren museum. Illustrated in that work is a neckrest carved by the same hand as the present example and collected in the Lusambo area by Dr. Maes himself (1929: plate VII, fig. 11). There is a second neckrest by the artist in the Tervuren collection, and a third in the collection of the Detroit Institute of Arts.

J. W. Mestach is currently studying the Songye, and has written: "This type of sculpture belongs to the Nsapo subgroup, which belongs to the Beneki group [who live in extreme southwest Songye country, near the Kasai Luba] of the Songye. This is why one can find these objects illustrated in catalogues attributed to three different groups. This very particular style must come, it seems to me, from a single workshop located in the Kananga (Luluabourg) region, where many ethnic groups of different origins have come into contact" (Mestach 1984).

This very distinctive style is characterized by the pinched facial features, the tiny mouth, the enormous eyes, the large domed forehead, and especially by the enormous, flat feet, carved in low relief on the base. This object, the neckrests from Tervuren and Detroit, as well as others from Italian museums and a large figure collected in 1907 for the Leipzig museum, have all been attributed to a "Master of Beneki."

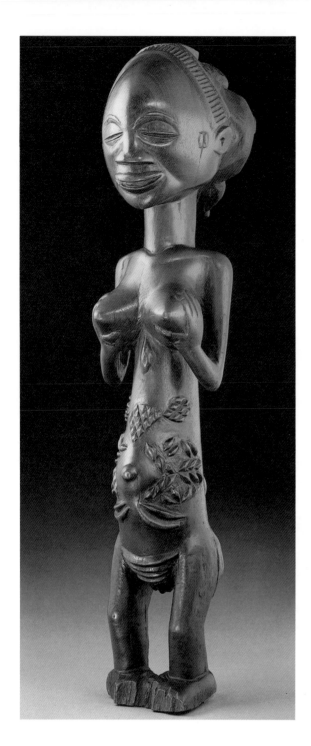

117. LUBA, Zaire / Female figure, *mikisi mihake* / Wood / H. 34.9 cm. (14")

"This standing female figure falls into the category of *mikisi mihake* (Colle 1913:435–6). *Mikisi* refers to a sculpted figure, and *mihake* to the medicinal ingredients a sorceror placed in the hole inside the head. Burton (1961:129) states that figures like this one served as guardians whose efficacy depended on their degree of refinement. Because only wealthy individuals could afford finely carved figures, this beautifully articulated sculpture must have belonged to a person of high social standing.

"'It is important to understand that royal women played a fundamental role in the expansion of the Luba Kingdom. They were sent to client chiefdoms as emissaries where they served as ambassadors, spies, and tribute collectors. Kings also frequently bestowed their sisters, wives, and daughters upon client chiefs as wives. Because most groups surrounding the patrilineal Luba were matrilineal, any child conceived through such a union had the right to local rule since he descended from his mother's side. This was an effective way

of integrating outlying groups into the political network without force' (Reefe 1981:133–5). The important role of women in Luba political structure may help to explain their prominent place in Luba art" (Nooter 1984a).

"This figure is a perfect example of the Luba 'Heartland' style. The Luba Heartland is the region which was the seat of central Luba authority from the seventeenth to the nineteenth centuries. It encompasses the area around Kamina and Kabongo in the Shaba District of southeastern Zaire (Reefe 1981:8; Maesen 1982: personal communication [with Nooter]). This figure's softly rounded forms, coffee-bean eyes, four-lobed coiffure, and scarification patterns all reflect the style of the Luba 'Heartland.' It is, however, difficult to assess the exact provenance of this piece because art objects were dispersed throughout the region by kings as tokens of respect. Furthermore, Luba art was so prestigious that surrounding groups frequently copied it (Maesen 1982: personal communication)" (Nooter 1984c).

118. LUBA, Zaire / Woman holding a bowl, *mboko* or *kitumpo kya muchi* / Wood / H. 28.6 cm. (11″)

The carved figure of a woman holding a bowl on her knees was called *mboko* by the Luba, and was used by diviners who placed white kaolin clay, *pemba*, in the bowl. During the investiture of a subordinate chief, the new ruler received some of the white clay which symbolized the major ancestral spirits. The clay was carried to the ruler's home village where it was stored in a bowl held by a female figure (Reefe 1981: 91). Diviners used the clay in containers representing a spirit. They applied some of the clay to their bodies before and after the divination process (Colle 1913:441). A means of divination practiced by medicine men is to place powdered chalk along with a variety of objects in a bowl. The bowl is shaken and seems to get heavier and heavier. The diviner calls out to the spirit to whom the bowl is dedicated to show him the cause of the troubles in question. The arrangement of the objects in the bowl provides the answer to the client's prob-

lems. A female figure bearing a bowl is called *kitumpa kya muchi*. The bowl usually has a lid on it, and the woman is usually pregnant. The necromancer's familiar spirit lives in the bowl. He sleeps with the bowl near his head and takes it with him on trips. He is the only person who calls the figure by its formal name—others call it *mboko* (Burton 1961: 58–9; Tatum 1984).

This very old example of the *mboko* has seen decades of use. The hands of numerous diviners have worn the surface of the face and back smooth, while during some period of neglect, a rat gnawed at the legs and feet. The woman's body is covered with raised patterns of scars and her hair is plaited into a large knot at the back of her head. She holds her bowl forward, offering the white clay of the spirits into the diviner's hands.

119. LUBA, Zaire / Ceremonial spear / Wood, iron, cloth / H. 156.2 cm. (61")

This old and finely crafted spear bears the figure of a woman wearing the scars and hairstyle of the Luba Heartland style. The heavy forged iron base permitted the spear to be thrust upright into the ground during investiture ceremonies. Polly Nooter (1984b) has recently studied the political regalia of the Luba and writes: "Spears are one of several types of objects which constitute the ruler's insignia. The other leadership objects are stools [catalogue no. 120, 121], staffs, bowstands [catalogue no. 122], knives, axes, and *mboko* or female figures holding cups [catalogue no. 118]. All of these ceremonial objects figured prominently in the ruler's investiture rites—rites which linked the new ruler to the mythical founders of the kingdom, and thereby legitimized his authority."

"Ceremonial spears were used in two episodes of the investiture ceremony. On the investiture day, after the ruler was ritually cleansed and freshly clothed, he was carried before the crowd on the shoulders of his first officer. Preceding him were his sister and first wife who carried the staff and the spear which they planted in the ground on either side of the

royal stool (Van Geluwe 1982: personal communication). After the investiture, the war dance, or *kutumboka*, began: the king was lifted onto a litter supported by the weapons of his most heroic soldiers and was carried around in triumphant procession while gongs sounded and the crowd joined in on the festivities. The dance symbolized the soldiers' will to support and defend the king throughout his reign (Theuws 1962:216; Van Avermaet 1954:709, 710; Burton 1961:23). This war dance is the reenactment of a mythical episode in which Kongolo (a cruel and incestuous despot) invites his nephew Kalala Ilunga (who seeks the throne and who ultimately becomes the first legitimate king of the Luba) to perform a dance over a concealed pit filled with spears. But Kalala Ilunga, who has been warned by a diviner, detects the pit with his own spear as he dances, and thus ruins Kongolo's plans for his destruction (Gohring 1970; Van Malderen 1936:177; Verhulpen 1936:182; Wydert 1938)" (Nooter 1984b and 1984c).

120. LUBA, Zaire / Royal stool / Wood / H. 52 cm. (20″)

Among the Luba and other groups throughout southeastern Zaire, stools were symbols of rank and prestige. Male heads of households had small, carefully carved stools, and rulers had large, impressive stools like this and the following example to elevate themselves above the level of the floor where lower ranks were seated. The female supporting-figures for these royal stools probably refer to the ruler's dependence on his female ancestors for the continuity of the royal lineage. One of the earliest visitors to the area was Cameron, who lived among the Luba from October, 1874 to June, 1875. He reported that: "When Kasongo sleeps at home, his bedroom furniture consists of members of his harem. Some on hands and knees form a couch with their backs, and others lying flat on the ground provide a soft carpet." Cameron also visited a Songye chief who used a Luba style stool: ". . . he brought a

large and handsomely carved stool, upon which he sat, while he used one of his wives who was seated on the ground as his footstool" (Cameron 1877 II : 16–18, 70). Among the Shankadi-Luba, a stool was an important element in the regalia of chiefs, and it was a crime for anyone but a chief to sit on a stool (Burton 1961 : 31). Joseph Cornet states that the stool is among the primary prestige objects. One of the wives of the chief is responsible for looking after it (Tatum 1984).

This stool, which has been damaged badly by insects, displays characteristics of the northern Luba style, closest to the Hemba across the Lualaba River to the east. The head is massive and fully rounded, with a high, domed forehead, and the hair is bound up in the distinctive cross shape that is so common in Hemba sculpture. When complete, the seat of the stool must have been three feet above the ground.

121. LUBA, Zaire / Royal stool / Wood / H. 37.5 cm. (15")

During his investiture, a Luba chief is given the seat of his counsellor (*kioni*) and is told "There is your throne; take it." The chief then sits between his counsellor and his niece (*mfinga*), in accordance with a Luba saying: "A niece to sleep with, a grandchild to fondle, and a grandmother to lean upon" (Burton 1969:22). Cameron reports that when a chief dies, "a woman is placed on her hands and knees, and upon her back the dead chief, covered with his beads and other treasures, is seated, being supported on either side by one of his wives, while his second wife sits at his feet" (Cameron 1877 II:333).

Jack Flam concludes from these descriptions that "the figure represented on [Luba] stools is not literally either a slave or a person of high rank, but is instead a compound symbol,

which refers to a founder of a tribe or a family. Among the matrilineally oriented BaLuba, the function of the stool can be seen quite clearly to be that of a symbolic statement of the continuance of power" (Flam 1970:56–7).

This beautiful small stool was collected by Cecil Rhodes at the end of the nineteenth century, and was given to the captain of the steamship on which he returned to England. The helmet shape of the face and heavy scarification on the body indicate that it was produced by the Luba Shankadi, in spite of the absence of a "cascade" hairstyle, which some authors have used erroneously as the determinant Shankadi characteristic.

SOUTHERN SAVANNAH: Sankuru/Lualaba Rivers/Lake Tanganyika Area

122. LUBA, Zaire / Bowstand / Wood, fiber / H. 65.1 cm. (26")

The bowstands of the Luba were described in the early literature by European visitors to southeastern Zaire. Father Colle
reported that bowstands could be made of either iron or wood.
They were placed next to the conjugal bed, and driven into
the ground or into the wall of the house (Colle 1913:167–8).
The arrows placed on the stand were symbols of marriage.
During the wedding ceremony an arrow is placed in the ground
before the parents of the bride and groom to symbolize the
indissoluble nature of the marriage (Sendwe 1955:61, Preeraer
and Manoly 1938:11). Others reported that the bowstand was
a symbol of chiefly power (de Maret 1973:10, Hall 1923:
192–197). The bowstand was placed before the chief to hold
his bow and arrows. A woman of high rank was the only person
allowed to care for the object (Cornet 1972:212, Tatum 1984).

Similar bowstands, made of iron, have been described among
the Bemba and other groups in northern Zambia west of Lake
Tanganyika, where they were called *nsakakabemba*. "These
bowstands are considered as sacred, because they are defi-
nitely considered to be relics from the past. In all three tribes
I mention—Babemba, Babisa, Baunga—the natives declare
emphatically that the arrowstands came from Lubaland, from
whence they trace their origin. They were carried with them,
they say, on their march into their present territory some time
during the beginning of the eighteenth century. It is for this
reason, they assert, that the *nsakakabemba* are kept sacred in
the tribal relic houses, with other objects of similar origin;
and, in the case of the Babisa and Baushi, placed with other
valuables, such as ivory tusks, on the graves of chiefs" (Richards 1935:31).

123. HEMBA, Zaire / Female torso / Wood, glass beads / H. 21.6 cm. (8½")

A number of style characteristics help identify this as the work of the Hemba, who live east of the Lualaba River, rather than that of the Luba, who live on the west bank. The shape of the head with its high, domed forehead, the very sharp, angular jawline, the long, elegant nose, and the elaborate, cross-shaped coiffure are all typical of the Hemba style.

This type of object is found throughout the Luba/Hemba/ Kusu/Bembe area of southeastern Zaire, both east and west of the Lualaba River. A very similar piece in the Tishman collection, also distinctively Hemba, has been described by Father Pierre Colle, and discussed in depth by Huguette Van Geluwe. Such torsos were originally mounted on a calabash in which magical materials were stored. These were the property of the *buhabo* society—*bugabo* among other groups. "The *Buhabo* maintained that its intention was to promote mutual aid, but the principal, if unavowed, goal was actually the enrichment of its members. By using aggressive methods including poisoning and murder and by preying on people's fear, gullibility,

and belief in sorcery, the *Buhabo* extorted payments from their victims . . . At the top of the [*Buhabo*] hierarchy was the grand master (*tata* or *kalunga muhabo*). One of his privileges was to be the guardian of the great material representation of the protective spirit of the *Buhabo*" (Van Geluwe in Vogel 1981:223–5).

The *kabwelulu* usually consisted of a wooden torso with holes pierced around the base so that it could be attached to a large calabash. Unlike many examples of this type, this figure has a large hole pierced through from the head down to the base, so that magical materials could be poured into the funnel-like top of the head and fall into the container below. In addition, this beautiful figure lacks the heavy crust of sacrificial and magical materials that originally covered the Tishman piece. Instead, the beautifully modelled body forms and the color-contrasts remain unobscured. We see what the artist originally intended his patrons to see.

124. HEMBA, Zaire / Mask, *ibombo ya soho* / Wood / H. 21.6 cm. (8½")

The Hemba are best known for their beautiful figures of chiefs (catalogue no. 125); these have been studied in detail by François Neyt. Hemba masks are less well known and we have only a few brief notes on their meaning. They may be called *soko mutu* (Neyt 1977:503, alternatively *suku muntu*), meaning "brother of man" in Swahili, or *ibombo ya soho* "monkey face" in KiHemba (Cornet 1978:310). Father Cornet indicates that they may not have been intended as face masks, but as belt masks worn at a dancer's waist. They are remarkable for their extreme stylization, their large, upward-slanting eyes; enormous, grinning mouth; and nose that projects downward like a hook.

This example is also illustrated in Neyt's study of the Hemba (1977:ill. 112–113).

125. HEMBA, Zaire / Male ancestor figure, *singiti* / Wood / H. 73.7 cm. (29″)

This serene and dignified figure was carved in the southern Hemba Niembo chiefdoms, east of the Lualaba River and north of the Luika (Neyt 1977 : 170,171, no. IV 8). Figures from this area are characterized by an ovoid head, elongated neck, large swelling abdomen, and squared shoulders. The delicate eyebrows are crescent-shaped, and the eyes are almost closed, contributing to the impression of composed serenity. Since the explorations of Robert Livingstone and V. L. Cameron in the late 1870's, the Hemba have been known for their beautiful complex hairstyles. The hair is built up in a cross-form at the back of the head, oiled, colored with red powder, and plaited on a framework of raffia.

The Hemba place wooden ancestor figures, called *singiti*, in small huts which protect the figures from the elements. Many of these huts contain several figures. "The figure expresses the dependence of the world of the living on that of the dead—and is thus a funerary and religious symbol—and indicates the ownership of the land and the possession of social authority, both of which are based on the organization of clans and lineages. Even the wood out of which many of these figures are carved, *iroko*, possesses a religious significance" (Neyt in Vogel 1981 : 217).

126. BANGUBANGU (pre-Bembe hunters), Zaire / Ancestor figure / Wood / H. 58.1 cm. (23")

In the past ten years a number of scholars have remarked on the strong similarities in figure carving styles among groups who inhabit the west shore of Lake Tanganyika, especially the Bembe, Boyo, northern Hemba, Holoholo, Binja, and Bangubangu. These groups produce ancestor figures with long, cylindrical torsos, squared shoulders, and massive heads. In all cases the forehead is fully rounded with high, arched brows and "coffee-bean" eyes, which in some cases become quite large. The elongation of the cheeks, the very high-set eyes, and the very low-set mouth emphasize the distinctive angular shape of the jaw and chin. The sharp jaw-line is further emphasized by dentate patterns which represent a stylized fringe of beard.

Research published recently by Professor Daniel Biebuyck indicates that this homogeneous style complex is the result of the presence in each of these ethnic groups of small subgroups of "pre-Bembe hunters," a people who originated in the mid-nineteenth century in the Lualaba River area and then moved, in several waves, into the areas occupied by heterogeneous chiefdoms west of the lake. "All groups had strongly advanced worship of the heroic ancestors (founders of large groups and leaders of the migrations) and of the epony-

mous founders of clans, lineages, and autonomous political entities" (Biebuyck 1981:56–7). These "pre-Bembe hunters" carried with them the tradition of carving wooden figures of the venerated ancestors. "As the hunting groups settled (e.g., near the lake where they found permanent food supplies) and consolidated their political systems, the sculptural traditions further developed and differentiated . . ." to reflect contact with new neighbors, including the Tabwa and the Luba (Biebuyck 1981:57).

"Among eastern Lega, Bembe, Boyo, and pre-Bembe hunters and fishermen, [the] ancestral cult occurs in different forms.

Ancestors . . . appear in dreams and prescribe a certain course of action; they activate nature spirits to strike the living with sickness and misfortune, or they directly cause the evils. If the will of the ancestor is not revealed immediately in dreams, it becomes known through divination . . . In the public ancestral cult, the Bembe address themselves to the founders of local lineage segments. Because of the heterogeneous composition of the village, there are generally several ancestor shrines depending on the number (and numerical strength) of recognized semiautonomous lineages settled in the village" (Biebuyck 1981:24–6).

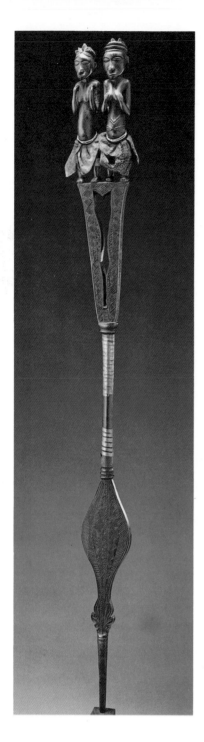 

127. HOLOHOLO, Zaire / Leadership staff / Wood, metal, cloth / H. 123.1 cm. (48½")

In 1979 I attributed this beautiful paddle-shaped staff to the Luba (Roy 1979a:183), but later Roy Sieber and I looked at it more carefully, and at his suggestion I compared it to objects in German collections. It became apparent that it should be assigned to the Holoholo on the basis of the shape of the faces, with their elongated, almond-shaped eyes and protuberant mouths. Three staves that are very close stylistically are illustrated in the catalogue of the Staatliches Museum für Völkerkunde in Munich (Kecskesi 1982:417, 418, 419), all collected by Arneth in 1909. A standing figure in Berlin was collected in 1907 by Schloifer (Krieger 1965:no. 244).

The similarities between the Luba and Holoholo styles is due to the domination of the Holoholo by the Luba, who penetrated to the shores of Lake Tanganyika in the reign of Ilunga Sungu (ca. 1780–1810). "Some Luba conquerors settled there among the Holoholo, an amalgam of local matrilineal peoples who had been living under Tumbwe domination. Lakeside populations around Kalemie and villagers living in the mountains behind them remained tributaries of the Luba royal court during the subsequent reigns of Kings Kumwimbe Ngombe and Ilunga Kabale" (Reefe 1981:124).

Decorated canoe paddles play an important role in the story of the founding of the Luba royal lineage. When Kongolo, the evil king, was defeated by Kalala Ilunga, the founder of the Luba royal lineage, he fled across the Lomami River. To the ferrymen who helped him across, he gave a canoe paddle decorated with figures and bound with copper. When Kalala Ilunga pursued Kongolo, he found another ferryman upstream from Kongolo's crossing, and gave him a decorated paddle as a reward for his help. Each river-crossing village claims to have one of the two original paddles of Kongolo and Kiluwe (Womersley 1984:12–15) (Tatum 1984).

128. KUSU, Zaire / Ancestor figure / Wood, beads, textile / H. 83 cm. (32½")

The Kusu live between the Lomami and Lualaba Rivers north of the Songye, east of the Tetela, and west of the Bembe, Boyo, and northern Hemba who inhabit the west shore of Lake Tanganyika.

Throughout this large area there has been a free exchange of sculptural influences and a sharing of object types. Many of these groups use large ancestor figures like this Kusu example and the Hemba (catalogue no. 125) and Bangubangu (pre-Bembe, catalogue no. 126) figures. In all three pieces we see a narrowing of the chest to provide space for the arms above the swelling abdomen. The neck is long and cylindrical, the head massive, its elegant, domed forehead heightened by shaving the hairline back to a line that passes from ear to ear over the top of the head.

While the face of a "classical" Hemba figure tends to be fully rounded, with a smooth transition from jaw to cheek, the Kusu style favors a more angular face. A sharp line marks the jaw; a small, pointed beard accentuates the triangular shape of the lower face. Also, the Kusu use much larger, protuberant, "coffee-bean" eyes. In addition, there are marked differences in hairstyles between the groups. The most remarkable characteristic of this Kusu figure is its heart-shaped face, clearly outlined by the graceful curve of the brows from the bridge of the nose to the jaw (compare with illustration XIV. 11 in Neyt 1981:272).

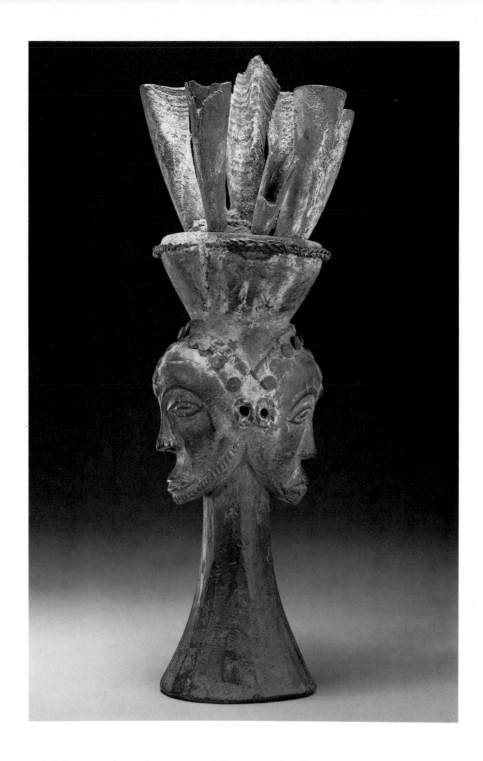

129. KUSU, Zaire / Magical figure with two faces / Wood, horn, metal tacks and nails, magical materials / H. 34.3 cm. (13½")

Here, as in the preceding figure, the Kusu style is characterized by the heart-shaped face with its long, triangular chin, by the slightly protuberant mouth, and by the eyes, typically almond-shaped and heavy-lidded. The male face has a fringe of beard and is, in style, very close to the Holoholo staff (catalogue no. 127).

By the addition of magical ingredients to the many antelope horns that project from the top of the head, this figure was endowed with supernatural power. The male/female pairing may refer to the protective power of the founding ancestral couple. Similar full figure Kusu and Hemba objects, called *kabeja*, prevent disease and malformations in infants, and protect the owner and his family by receiving sacrifices to their ancestral spirits.

130. TABWA, Zaire / Figure / Wood / H. 41.9 cm. (16½")

The Tabwa live in extreme southeast Zaire, on the west shore
of Lake Tanganyika. The Tumbwe live to the north, and the
Bemba to the south in Zambia. The Hemba are to the west.

   This male ancestor figure belongs to Style I, the "Classic
Tabwa Style," as defined by Bernard de Grunne in a thesis on
Tabwa sculpture. The "Classic" traits include the forked bird-
claw ("patte-d'oie") scars at the corners of the eyes; large,
round eyes; an open mouth with the tongue protruding
slightly; and a long, pendulant hairstyle. Other figures in this
group are in the collection of the Royal Museum for Central Africa, Tervuren (no. 50.18.1) and the British Museum
(no. 14.056). The present example is remarkable for its beau-

tiful, long hairstyle: note the delicate patterns around a
diamond-shaped center, which hangs far down the back.

   Such objects were used in the cult of ancestors (*mipasi*):
"These are portraits of ancestors who founded the clan or who
had an important role to play in the history of the clan . . .
The role of the ancestor statues was to protect the village
and especially the chief, who is generally a descendant of the
person represented [by the figure]. The statuettes were placed
in huts of the same form as those in which the BaTabwa live,
but of much smaller size . . . These huts are usually found
near the home of the chief . . ." (de Grunne 1980a: 105–6).

131. TABWA, Zaire / Mask / Wood / H. 32.4 cm. (12¾")

Very little is known about the various types and functions of Tabwa masks. In his thesis on the Tabwa, Bernard de Grunne included illustrations of two masks. One, a naturalistic helmet mask, called *moussangwe* (H. Kamer collection), may be of the same type as this example. The second is a buffalo mask, called *kiyounde*, now in the collection of Jean Paul Barbier in Geneva and illustrated in William Fagg's catalogue of that collection's masks (Fagg 1980 : 152–3). The Fagg catalogue includes a photograph by Marc Felix of the buffalo mask in action.

According to de Grunne, the human mask, including this example, represents the female character, and the buffalo mask represents the male character. Together, the two form a mask pair which is used in fertility rites for sterile women. As part of the rite, the women are forced to drink some of the sap of the tree (*Erythrina abyssinica*) from which the masks are carved (Fagg 1980 : 152; de Grunne 1980a : 46).

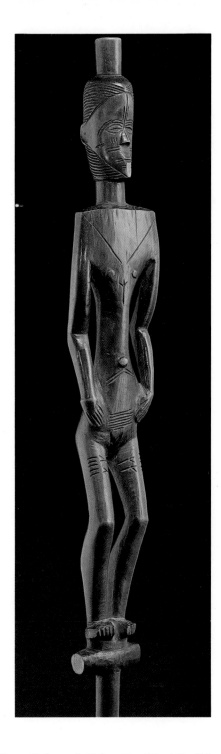

132. MALUNGU (Marungu, BaMarungu, Bena Malungu), Zaire, Zambia / Staff figure / Wood / H. 48 cm. (19")

The Malungu (or Marungu) live at the extreme southern tip of Lake Tanganyika in Zambia. A small portion of the population inhabits the corner of Zaire, between the border and the west shore of the lake, but all the Malungu belong to G. P. Murdock's Bemba Cluster of the Central Bantu. The Tabwa live just to the north, and the Bemba to the south.

With the Tabwa and the Bemba the Malungu form a stylistic transition from the styles of Eastern Zaire to the art of eastern Africa. The Malungu style itself is a combination of Tabwa and Bemba elements, most clearly seen in the scarification patterns beneath the eyes, which are characteristically Bemba, and in the concentric patterns around the eyes, which are similar to Tabwa, Bemba, and Holoholo style traits. Also, the elaborate scars on the chest and abdomen are very similar to the scars on Tabwa figures.

The object seems to have formed the decoration of the upper portion of a staff, perhaps a leadership staff like those used by groups to the east, especially the Luba.

EAST AFRICA

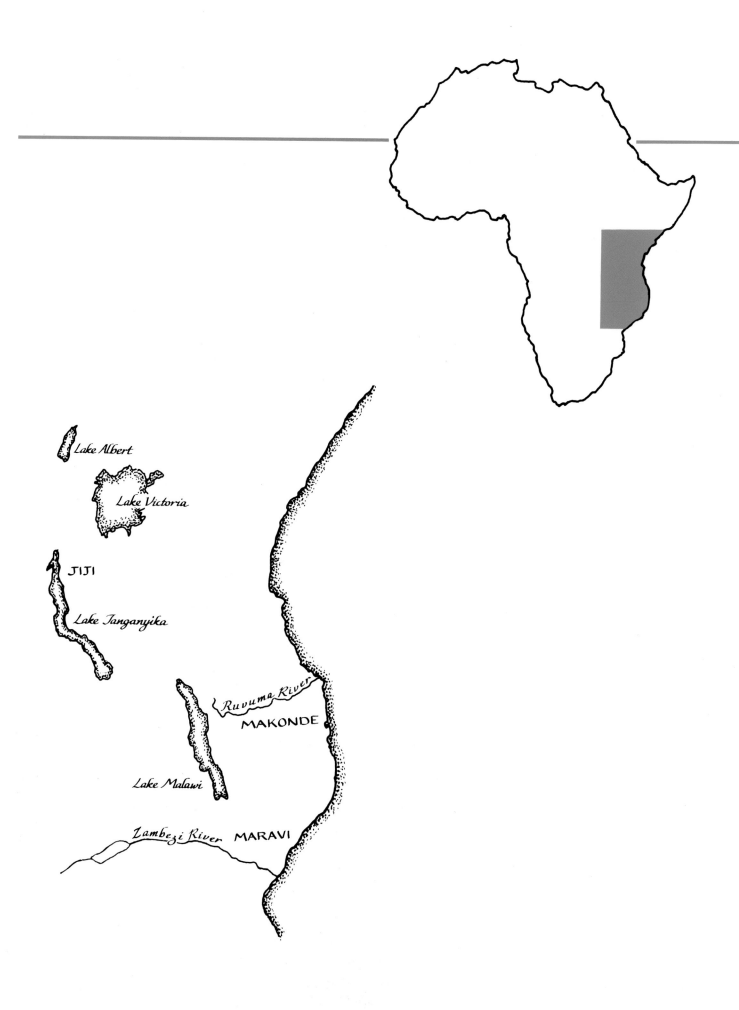

Lake Albert

Lake Victoria

JIJI

Lake Tanganyika

Ruvuma River

MAKONDE

Lake Malawi

Zambezi River MARAVI

The East African Style Area

The East African style area comprises the area between the great chain of Lakes Albert, Edward, Kivu, Tanganyika, Mweru, and Malawi, and the Indian Ocean. In the south is the Limpopo River, and in the north the Tana River. This is a dry area of broad grassy high plains, populated by pastoralists, interspersed with cool wet highlands where agriculture is possible.

The major cultivated crops are corn, beans, cassava, sorghum and bananas. Important cash crops, introduced by Europeans, are tobacco, sugar, coffee, and tea.

The Arab-African Swahili culture that developed along the coast during the long period of the Indian Ocean slave trade was the major intrusive factor before the arrival of the Portuguese at the end of the fifteenth century, and of the English and Germans in the nineteenth century. From about 1000 to 1500 A.D. the Shona miners of Zimbabwe sold their gold along the coast of Mozambique to Swahili and Indian seafaring merchants. In about the twelfth century the Shona built a number of important cities out of stone, including Great Zimbabwe, and in the mid-fifteenth century they founded the Monomotapa Empire, which was eclipsed by the Rozvi Empire from the seventeenth to the end of the eighteenth century.

The scattered and idiosyncratic styles of East Africa are difficult to sort into style areas. Ladislav Holy (1967) divided the area we are concerned with here into two major style areas: "Central East Africa" including groups between Lake Tanganyika and the Indian Ocean, and "Southern East Africa" including the Makonde, Yao, Chemba and Maravi between Lake Malawi and the coast. Each of these large areas was broken down into numerous substyles. The styles of the central area, closely related to the sculptural forms of extreme eastern Zaire, are characterized by cylindrical torsos and necks and large, spherical heads marked by rows of incised patterns. The styles of the southern area are more naturalistic and fully rounded, with lip labrets, scarification patterns formed of wax or chip-carved, and the frequent use of glued-on human hair. Although the best-known style is that of the Makonde, other groups seem to conform to these traits. As studies devoted solely to East African sculpture become available in the future, it will be possible to refine this style classification scheme.

133. JIJI, Tanzania and Burundi / Staff / Wood / H. 43.2 cm. (17″)

A number of groups have been suggested as the source of this small and delicate staff. The full, round head, protuberant mouth, and concentric almond-shaped eyes resemble the styles of groups west of Lake Tanganyika, including the Tabwa, Holoholo, and Bemba. However, the attenuation of body forms suggests a group farther east, perhaps the Jiji, who live on the eastern shore of the lake, an area which forms a transitional zone from eastern Zaire to the sculptural styles of East Africa. The distinctive angular shape of the lower legs may ultimately provide a clue.

The figure is seated with the hands in front of the umbilicus. A snake wraps itself around the staff just below the feet, and the sphere above the head is hollowed to form a very small bowl that may once have held snuff, although it shows little sign of wear. The staff is far smaller than the leadership staffs of such eastern Zaire groups as the Luba.

134. MARAVI, Mozambique / Female figure / Wood, metal, beads / H. 25.5 cm. (10")

The Maravi live along the lower Zambezi River, south of Lake Malawi, in Mozambique. They belong to G. P. Murdock's "Maravi Cluster" of the Central Bantu, which also includes the Chewa, Nyasa, Zimba, and Kunda.

Maravi sculpture has often been misattributed to the Makonde, who live near the coast in northern Mozambique, because both groups wear and represent in their sculpture the large ornamental lip labret. This figure, and others attributed to the Maravi, bears distinctive bands of chip-carved triangles across the chest and abdomen. Such marks do not appear on

Makonde figures, but do appear on objects from the Bemba and Lomwe south of Lake Malawi (see Holy 1967:no. 115 for an example of Maravi sculpture in Berlin). A figure very similar to this one in size, style, and pose is illustrated by William Fagg (1970:99, no. 110) who indicates that it was collected "within the territory of the WaGindo," and that the decorative patterns are the result of Arab influence.

The literature published about this area offers no clue as to the function of this figure.

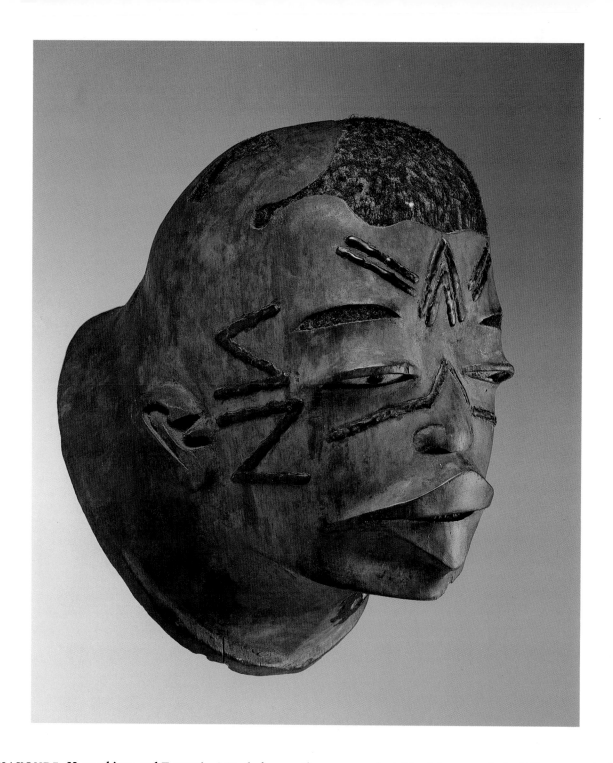

135. MAKONDE, Mozambique and Tanzania / Mask, for *mapiko* masquerade / Wood, beeswax, hair / H. 25.4 cm. (10″)

The Makonde are best known for their masks representing human and animal characters. Two major styles exist: rather abstract face masks that were collected in large numbers by German colonials in what is now Tanzania, and more naturalistic helmet masks, like this one, that were produced by the Makonde living in Mozambique. These masks are associated with male and female initiations. The German ethnographer Karl Weule, who, just after the turn of the century, collected most of the masks that are now in German museums, reported that male and female masks were used to celebrate the emergence of young women from initiation camps. "The four masks . . . stand up two and two, each pair facing the other, and begin the same series of movements . . . The masks are of wood, two of them representing men, and two women. This is evident a hundred paces off, from the prominence given to the *pelele* [lip labret], whose white stands out with great effect from the rigid black surface" (Weule 1909:235). Jorge and Margot Dias have studied the

Makonde over the past thirty years and indicate that masks are worn in *mapiko* dances associated with the initiation of both men and women. Initiation includes instruction in the skills of adulthood, as well as in Makonde dances, songs, and the costumes and secrets of the *mapiko* masks. The initiates are told that the masks are not the spirits of the dead, but are worn by living men, and after a period of training in dance, they wear the masks in a great festival at the center of the village. The masks may also appear during an *ngoma* ceremony in which adolescents are taught about marriage and the demands of adult family life (Dias 1961:31, 46, 57–60; Dias and Dias 1964:56–81; 1970:159–217).

Makonde artists add to the naturalism of their carvings by using beeswax and human hair to represent scarification patterns and fashionable hairstyles. Many of the female masks include the large lip labrets that Makonde women used to wear.

CATALOGUE OF THE
1992 EXHIBITION

ELIZABETH MABEL HOLTHUES STANLEY

1906–1990

TO BETTY STANLEY

Betty Stanley began collecting African art in 1960, an extension of her long-standing interest in the arts. Although in the 1970s and early 1980s Max was more involved in expanding their African art collection, Betty played an important role in this effort. Max never bought an object without consulting her. When dealers visited Muscatine, Max would select up to ten objects, have them placed on the dining room table, and ask Betty what she thought about them. Although her reaction to a piece sometimes dissuaded him from purchasing it, more frequently she encouraged him to acquire fine pieces, and when his checkbook could no longer stand the strain, Betty began to make purchases herself. One of her most notable acquisitions is the small bronze horse and rider from the Inland Delta of the Niger; Betty bought it in 1983 at a time when Max had exhausted his budget. After Max's death in New York in the fall of 1984, this and several other objects Betty had purchased came to The University of Iowa.

For the first year after Max passed away, Betty showed no interest in collecting. In late 1985, however, following the exhibition *Art and Life in Africa: Selections from the Stanley Collection*, she began to purchase a few objects from two or three dealers with whom she and Max had had particularly warm relationships. One of the earliest and most important purchases was the outstanding Lele mask, illustrated on the cover of this catalogue, which was acquired from Jacques Hautelet. By far the greatest number of fine objects was purchased from the Belgian dealer Marc Félix. Betty and Max had visited Félix in Brussels, and he visited Muscatine two or three times a year. Betty was fond of Marc and eventually would purchase almost exclusively from him. Marc would sometimes give her objects (especially ones she did not find appealing) because he felt they would find a good home at The University of Iowa.

Betty felt that there were significant gaps in the collection that Max might have filled, and she strove to do this as well as acquire objects that marked an improvement in quality over ones the university already owned. To distinguish her purchases from Max's for the sake of student research in the years to come, she agreed that the objects she bought from 1985 on would be marked with "EMS" (Elizabeth Mabel Stanley) rather than with the "CMS" (Claude Maxwell Stanley) used for the earlier part of the collection, but that the numbering would continue in sequence. Max's last purchase was numbered CMS 599 (CMS 598, a Chokwe mask, and CMS 599, a Bete mask, had been selected by Max at Pace Gallery just hours before he died); Betty's first piece, a Woyo pot lid given to her by Marc Félix, was numbered EMS 600. Betty's last purchase was EMS 733, a Pende mask.

Betty acquired some of the most important objects in the Stanley Collection. She considered her most important purchases to be the Boa mask, which in her home was always placed next to a large Picasso print from the late 1930s; the Tsaam (or Mbala) drummer and the red Biombo mask, both of which had been collected in Zaire by Leo Frobenius; and the Lele mask. Although Betty purchased fewer objects than her husband did, in quality the scupture she acquired was equal to the best of Max's purchases. She was more willing than he to purchase objects that were needed to fill gaps even if they did not appeal to her personally, and she made fewer errors because she rarely purchased without considerable expert advice. Like Max, however, she had sufficient breadth of mind to understand peoples whose way of life and thought were enormously different from her own. She too was motivated by an abiding eagerness to change the parochial attitudes she felt some Americans had about the character and quality of life in Iowa. She was proud of Iowa, of The University of Iowa, and of the contribution she and Max were able to make to the understanding of African art and life.

Those who knew Betty even slightly will remember her warm and gentle smile. At the Iowa exhibitions and conferences in 1985 and 1987, she struck up friendships with a number of the participants and hosted the banquets following the conferences. The many Africanists who met her were charmed by her warmth and put at ease by her kind manner. To them and to all who are interested in the art and life of Africa, she also leaves a legacy of a comprehensive vision and a generous spirit.

Christopher D. Roy

WESTERN SUDAN

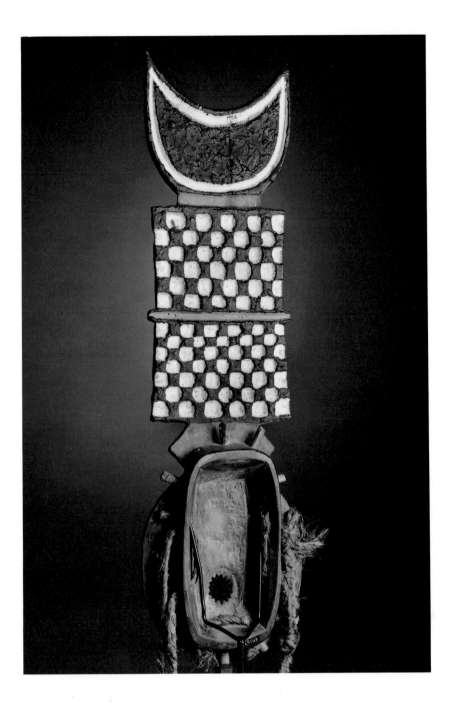

1. BWA, Burkina Faso / Mask, *luruya* / Wood, fiber / H. 81.3 cm. (32")

This mask represents a dwarf ancestor of the Bwa. It is a small version of the great plank masks for which the southern Bwa are famous.

The elders of the Bondé family in Boni tell the story of an ancestor who remained the size of a small child throughout his long life. As he grew up, he acquired magical powers to talk with the animals in the wild bush that surrounded the village. On his deathbed, he asked his family to remember him after death with a small mask identical in every detail to the great plank masks that the other men of the family wore at initiations and funerals.

This mask is notable for the depth of the carving of scarification patterns, which are similar to those worn by the Bwa themselves. Such deeply carved patterns are typical of very old masks that were carved by the most skilled Bwa artists.

EQUATORIAL FOREST

2. BEKOM, Cameroon / Mask / Wood, copper / H. 39.7 cm. (15⅝")

Masks similar to this one, covered with a thin sheet of copper appliqué and brass upholstery tacks, were kept in the royal storerooms of the Fon, the ruler of the kingdom of Kom. According to Pierre Harter (1986: 218), this type was called *akam*, and was worn on top of the performer's head facing upward, together with a costume of blue-and-white cloth imported from the Benue River valley.

Writing of the nearby Bamum kingdom, Geary states:

Every Bamum stood in a pyramidal dependency relationship to the king which was visually expressed by the anthropomorphic masks'

bowing before the king. Such an interpretation of the masquerade stresses the symbolic reproduction of social and political structure. (Geary 1983: 134)

This was a very important mask type, worn by the chief dancer of the king's court. During celebrations, the dancer wearing this mask would lead a long procession of several distinctive mask types across the plaza in front of the palace.

3. TOGBO, Zaïre / Figure / Wood, metal, fiber, coins / H. 27.7 cm. (10⅞")

This small figure is from the Togbo, who live just to the east of the Bwaka, south of the Ubangi River in northwest Zaïre. The armless cylindrical torso, the use of blue beads (in this case as eyes), and the attaching of numerous rings and coins to the figure are similar to style conventions among peoples farther east, especially the Azande. The large ears and pinched face, however, are uniquely Togbo characteristics (Maes 1938: Pl. XXVII, figs. 1, 2, 3). The Togbo may have intended these figures to represent the creator-being Ngakola.

Ngakola is the representative of the supreme being, who is responsible for good and evil, called on at every occasion, whether to gain a favor or to avoid a disaster. This belief is habitually exploited by magicians who attribute mysterious powers to their idols, for which they blame any failed enterprise that would have been guaran-teed success, and to acquire the blessings of Ngakola offerings are multiplied. The wife of Ngakola holds the power to impregnate women said to be sterile and to ease the pain of childbirth. Some elders claim to have heard Ngakola, for to look on him will cause blindness. (Glenisson, quoted in Maes 1938: 124)

Godefroid also writes that larger representational female figures were carved to avert warfare between two villages that might result from the murder of someone from a distant village by a member of a Togbo community. Small figures were carved to represent the child desired by an infertile woman. The figure was placed in bed beside the woman, who prayed for a similar child. Later the figure would be placed in a cradle next to the newborn infant (quoted in Maes 1939: 160–61).

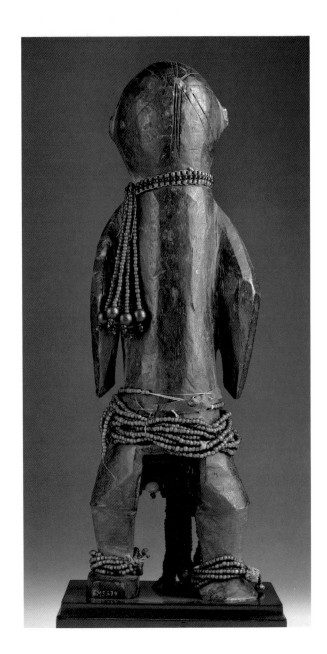

4. MANJA, Zaire and Central African Republic / Male figure / Wood, beads / H. 32.8 cm. (12⅞")

The Manja people live in the Central African Republic and northwestern Zaire, south of the great bend in the Ubangi River and east of Bangui. They are a Sudanese people whose legends describe repeated migrations south, perhaps to escape slave traders. As they moved south, they settled among the peoples already inhabiting the Ubangi area, especially the Ngbaka and Ngbandi. Their migration was complete by the time Europeans arrived late in the nineteenth century.

This figure may represent a specific ancestor spirit called Ngakola, who, with his wife Ngandala and daughter Yamisi, formerly lived in the Manja world. Ngakola had dark skin covered with long hair and possessed the power to give and take life.

Very few Manja sculptures are found in African art collec-

tions. There are marked similarities between the styles of the Manja and their Ngbaka and Ngbandi neighbors, especially in the use of broad, geometric volumes. Whereas the Ngbaka and Ngbandi use a heart-shaped face, the Manja more frequently use tangent circles to form the orbits and cheeks. Manja figures and masks usually lack the strong ridge of scars typical of the figures of neighboring peoples, including the Ngbaka and Ngbandi.

A figure virtually identical to this one, collected in 1913 by Larsonneur, is in the Museum für Völkerkunde in Berlin. In 1920 Charles Ratton purchased this figure from the Capitan Collection, and it remained in his collection until it was sold some years ago. It was purchased by Betty in 1986.

5. NGBAKA (Bwaka, Bouaka, Gbaya, M'Baka), Zaire / Female figure / Wood / H. 19 cm. (7½")

Large figures such as the Ngbaka figure in the Stanley Collection (no. 69 in the 1985 exhibition) may represent founding ancestors or creator deities, but it is likely that small figures like this one were used in private magical ceremonies to benefit an individual or his or her family. Small figures from the Manja, who live east and south of the Ngbaka, are used in this way.

6. LOBALA, Zaire / Drum / Wood / H. 71.2 cm. (28"); L. 317 cm. (105")

The Lobala live along the eastern bank of the Ubangi River just upstream from its confluence with the main course of the Zaire (Congo) River. The Bwaka people live to the north, and the Ngala to the south. The area between the two great rivers is low and marshy, and seems to have been chosen by the Lobala for defensive purposes.

The Lobala are known for their enormous ideophones, slit-gongs carved in the form of animals. Drums were used to call people to meetings and send messages over long distances. One early visitor wrote in 1911 that in the still of dusk the sound of such a drum could be heard fifteen kilometers away.

In this piece, the head of a powerful bush buffalo projects from the enormous body of the drum. The horns curve backward and down as the animal curls its upper lip and raises its tail, frozen in an eternal threat to charge. The two sides, or lips, of the drum were carved to different thicknesses to produce different tones when they were struck in alternation with a wooden mallet.

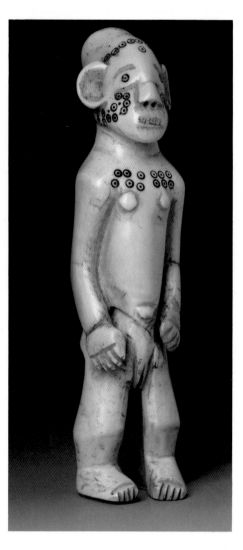
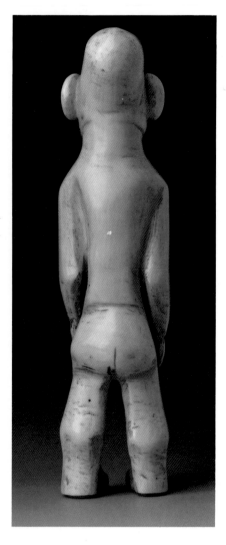

7. MANGBETU, Zaire / Male and female pair / Ivory / H. 21 cm. (8¼")

The Mangbetu have become famous for their refined representations of human figures that decorated objects like pipes, jars,
and musical instruments, and occasionally were carved as full-
length figures. All of these objects date from the period following the arrival of Belgian colonials; they were almost certainly
made to sell to the Belgians to secure cash to pay taxes. In
addition, a large number of objects were made for the American explorer Herbert Lang, who collected for the American
Museum of Natural History in the winter of 1910.

Although Mangbetu figures in wood, including the large

figure in the Stanley Collection, are well known, figures in
ivory as large as these are exceedingly rare. This pair exhibits
the elongation of the head characteristic of most Mangbetu
sculpture, as well as patterns of circles and dots representing
the delicate tracings of dye the Mangbetu applied to their
bodies before important public spectacles.

This pair was acquired from the estate of Count Lippens, in
Belgium, and was probably collected by him in the first quarter of the twentieth century, when he was a senior colonial
official in the Belgian Congo.

8. BOA, Zaire / Mask / Wood / H. 23.2 cm. (9⅛")

The Boa originated west of the Zaire River. During the eighteenth century they migrated east toward the Mbomu River. In the nineteenth century they were attacked by Azande invaders but successfully resisted Azande domination. The Boa were known as excellent warriors, but after 1910 Christian missionaries succeeded in destroying the last remnants of tribal unity (Vansina 1966).

The masks of the Boa are extremely rare and have been widely copied. Although most published examples are painted with broad patterns of black and white, only three—this one, a very similar mask in the collection of the Art Institute of Chicago, and an example in the Royal Museum of Central Africa—have such enormous ears.

The oval form of the mask is emphasized by the high forehead and the large, flaring pierced ears that jut out perpendicularly from the sides of the face. The large round eyes, the open mouth with its inset teeth of cane, and the pattern of large black and white geometric shapes add to the drama of the mask.

Although the use and function of the masks are unknown, they are usually described as war masks that belonged to secret societies or warriors' societies. They have also been described as disguises for hunting monkeys, although their dramatic forms would hardly have offered much reassurance to prey.

9. KOMO, Zaire / Mask / Wood, pigment / H. 31.2 cm. (12¼")

The Komo (Kumu, Bakumu, Bakumbu) live just to the north-west of the Lega in eastern Zaire. They share many social and cultural characteristics with the Lega and their other neighbors, including an emphasis on the importance of male initiation.

According to De Mahieu (quoted in Biebuyck 1986, 2: 234), these masks are called *nsembu* and are quite rare among the Komo, certainly rarer than among the Lega. They may be "archetypes of the initiator and his wife." A pair of masks, male and female, are used in ceremonies performed by diviners (*babankundu*). The male mask, *biangolo*, and the female mask, *ibole*, represent the father and mother of Ongondo, the uninitiated neophyte. The masks were owned by the elder men of the association of diviners (*nkunda*). They were used only at a diviner's initiation rites, usually held in conjunction with the funeral of a senior colleague.

According to Moeller (quoted in Biebuyck 1986, 2: 235) and Félix (pers. comm. 1987), the masks are wrapped in bark cloth and carried to the village of the new initiate. There, in a night-time ceremony, the performers who will wear the masks are dressed inside a house with a conical roof topped by the carved figure of a bird. The house is decorated with carved and painted wooden panels and painted doors. The masked performers, accompanied by assistants, emerge from the house to the accompaniment of horns. Their costumes of bark cloth and cane cover their arms and legs. They are seated on a bench, where they move their heads and arms to impersonate the living. Biebuyck notes that these traditions are very similar to those involving the large Lega masks called *muminia*, which perform from a seat in a corner of the initiation house.

Masks like this one are extremely rare. It was collected in the 1930s, perhaps by King Leopold III on a trip he made to eastern Zaire. It was brought to the United States by an American friend of Leopold who had accompanied him on the expedition.

10. HUNDE, Zaire / Altar post / Wood / H. 68.5 cm. (27")

The Hunde live between lakes Kivu and Eduard, southwest of the Rwanda and southeast of the Nyanga. The Lega live a short distance to the southwest and may have had a strong influence on Hunde political structure and art. The most widely cited evidence for this influence is an ivory figure of a woman, carved in the Lega style, that was collected in the Hunde village of Muvugni before 1913 by the explorer Rochette and is now in the Royal Museum of Central Africa, Tervuren. This altar post, one of the very few objects ever collected from the Hunde, demonstrates clearly that their art has style characteristics quite independent of the Lega. Its style is more closely associated with the Komo and other peoples of the Manyema area west of Lake Tanganyika. According to Félix, who collected this object, it was a post representing the primordial ancestors, carried in dances and placed on an altar when not in use.

11. NYINDU, Zaire / Mask / Wood / H. 26.5 cm. (10½")

This small, very old mask is in a number of respects similar to masks of the Bembe people on the western shore of Lake Tanganyika; the use of red and white pigment and the concave orbits of the eyes are typical of the *alunga* masks and figures of the Bembe. However, according to Marc Félix, who has recently published a study of the styles of the Manyema area west of Lake Tanganyika, the two-dimensional quality of the object and the arrangement of the red and white pigments in quadrants are more typical of the Nyindu people, who live just to the northwest of the Bembe and east of the Lega (Félix 1989: 94–103).

The Nyindu have been heavily influenced by both their Lega neighbors, with whom they share the important *bwami* society, and the Bembe, with whom they share the *alunga* cult of forest spirits. This is almost certainly a forest spirit mask from the area under Bembe influence.

SOUTHERN SAVANNAH

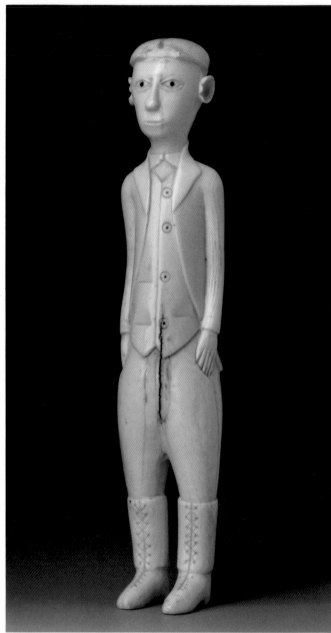

12. UNKNOWN PEOPLE, Zaire / Figure / Ivory / H. 22.3 cm. (8¾")

Betty Stanley formed a small collection of colonial period objects that had been produced for Europeans. Among her favorites was this beautifully carved figure of a European, complete with vest, jacket, shoes, and billed cap. The figure stands in a relaxed pose with his hands in his pockets. The straight hair indicates that it was not intended as a portrait of an African in European dress. The figure was produced by an unknown African artist in western Zaire in the 1920s, and it reflects the African artist's view of the stranger, the Other, in the colonial African world.

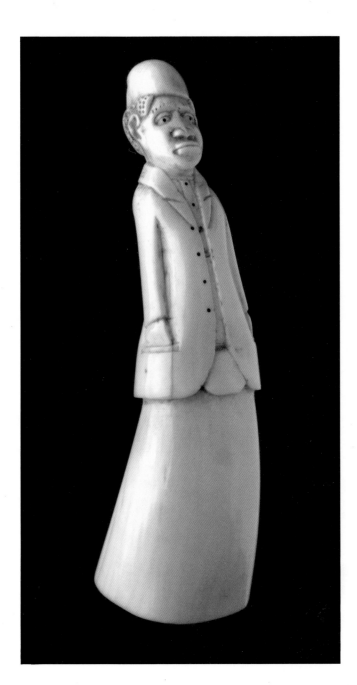 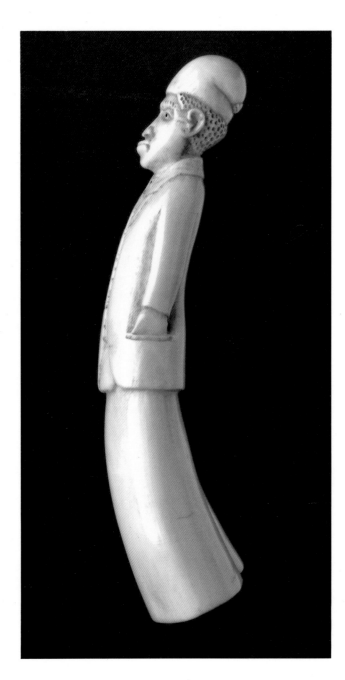

13. SALONGO, Zaire / Figure / Ivory / H. 12.1 cm. (4¾")

In contrast to no. 12, a much larger example, this tiny figure of hippopotamus ivory depicts a chief from Lower Zaire in the tasseled cap, European-style jacket, and wrapper that, for a local African of some stature, were considered acceptable dress by both colonials and the local population. Such objects were produced in large numbers by the Salongo people in the Lower Zaire River area late in the nineteenth century. They were intended to be prestige objects, whether owned by African political leaders or Belgian colonials. Like many images of outsiders or produced for outsiders, the object shows a degree of naturalism and a level of social commentary that are otherwise rare in African art. The details of the carving are so fine that the figure even seems to bear the perplexed expression of someone who has been forced to deal with the Belgian colonial administration.

14. SUKU, Zaire / Initiation mask, *kakungu* / Wood, raffia / 66 cm. (26")

The Suku use a variety of mask types in rituals at the young men's initiation camp, called *nkanda*. Large masks like this one are worn by the adult leader and charm specialist (*kisidika*); smaller masks (*kholuka*) are worn by the initiates themselves. Masks of this *kakungu* type are considered to be the oldest and most powerful of mask-charms (Bourgeois 1980: 42). The *kakungu*, a male version of the mask, is always accompanied by the female *kazeba*. They are usually painted dark reddish-brown and have a high forehead and drooping, inflated cheeks. Both *kakungu* and *kazeba* were worn with thick fiber costumes called *futi* or *kindua*, which also included animal skins.

Within *nkanda* initiation, the *kakungu* mask customarily appeared on the day of circumcision, the day of departure from the

nkanda camp, and occasionally for the subsequent breaking of food restrictions. Its appearance served to frighten the young candidates into obedience and respect for their elders, and to threaten any person secretly harboring evil intentions against one of the initiates. . . . The general function stated for *kakungu*, however, was to prevent witches, the *baloki*, from entering the camp and causing harm to the initiates, and for this purpose the mask was often kept in a special shelter within or near the initiation site. (Bourgeois 1980: 42–43)

Among the mask's reputed skills was the ability to jump enormous distances—e.g., over cabins or into the middle of the forest from the village—in seconds.

15. YAKA, Zaire / Initiation mask, *kholuka* / Wood, vegetable fiber, split cane, feathers, raffia / H. 66 cm. (26")

Large, dramatic masks like this first attracted the attention of collectors and students of African art to the Yaka. The most numerous Yaka mask types are those intended to be worn by adolescents and their tutors, which were exhibited to the public in dance spectacles celebrating the closing of the ordeal of circumcision, or *mukanda*.

Sexuality seems to play an important role in the function of these types of masks. In the context of circumcision, the mask provides protection to the young initiate in his transition to adulthood by shielding him from possible dangers in his life. These dangers include initial contacts with women, in which case it also serves to protect the future fertility of the initiated individual. *Kholuka* masks frequently have a multilayered construction surmounted by small figures. These human and animal figures represent sexuality and procreativity, and are

the subjects of stories that are part of the ceremonies. The animals play no specific role on their own, but become objects of explicit sexual meaning when the dancers sing verses that explain them (Bourgeois 1980: 5).

The very typical turned-up nose may also be a display of subtle phallicism. Renaat Devisch suggests a relationship between this nose and an elephant's trunk, which for the Yaka is a phallic symbol of procreation and in *mukanda* is associated with a fertility charm planted in front of the building in which masks are stored (1972: 155). This theory is supported by Adelman, who describes adolescent girls teasing "the boys before their initiation saying in effect that 'one does not know he has a nose until it hurts,' [referring] to their upcoming operation and suggesting that the nose may in fact serve as phallic symbol" (1975: 42).

16. ZOMBO, Zaire / Figure / Wood / H. 36 cm. (14¼")

The Zombo, who speak KiKongo, live in western Zaire, between the Yaka and the Kongo. The Holo, Songo, and Chokwe live nearby to the south. Stylistically the Zombo are part of the Yaka/Teke/Nkanu complex, but their figural works, like other objects from the area, show marked Chokwe influence, especially in the sunken orbits with bulging pupils, the narrow nose, the broad, downturned mouth, and the pattern incised in

the forehead. This figure's long torso narrowing into a columnar neck and its pose are comparable to those of the large Yaka figure in the Stanley Collection (no. 88 in the 1985 exhibition).

Like most other figures of similar pose and size, this was a power figure, used to cure affliction and to ward off evil. It was collected by a Belgian colonial officer in the northeastern Zombo area, near the Suku and Holo, before 1930.

17. PENDE, Zaire / Mask, *mbuya* / Wood, fiber, pigment / H. 30 cm. (11⅞")

Among the Western Pende along the Kwango River in central Zaire, masks are worn to celebrate the graduation of young men from the *mukanda* initiation camps, where they are taught the skills needed for survival and the responsibilities of adult men in village society. Skits or plays are staged that re-create the virtues and vices of well-known members of the community, including the buffoon (*tundu*), the epileptic (*mbangu*), the flirtatious girl (*gabuku*), and the chief (*fumu* or *ufumu*), who can be recognized by the pointed hairstyle we see here. All of the initiation masks, called *mbuya*, have a down-cast expression and an upturned nose. The sharp teeth are a mark of beauty, produced by chipping with a knife blade struck by a mallet.

In style this mask is quite different from the masks of the Eastern or Kasai Pende, who have been influenced by the Lele and other peoples in the confluence of the Kasai and Sankuru. The Western Pende have relationships with the Yaka and Suku to the west, as well as the Chokwe to the south. The upturned nose is an element taken from the Yaka, and the unbroken black line of the brows is a stylistic link to the Chokwe.

18. PENDE, Zaire / Mask / Wood, vegetable fiber, cloth / H. 16.2 cm. (6⅜")

This small wooden mask originated among the Eastern or Kasai Pende. According to Marc Félix, who collected it, masks of this type and style are worn only in the western part of the Kasai Pende area.

This type of mask is not illustrated in de Sousberghe's classic study (1958) of the Pende, or at least is difficult to associate with an illustrated type, so we know very little about its use or meaning. We may presume that it was used in initia-tions; it probably represents one of the many characters in the Pende community that appear in skits performed by recently initiated boys. The elaborate headgear of fiber and cloth, which constitutes the largest portion of the composition, makes this piece unusual among Pende masks in collections outside of Africa. The materials, colors, and patterns of this crest are evidence of the close cultural ties between the Kasai Pende and the Chokwe just to the south.

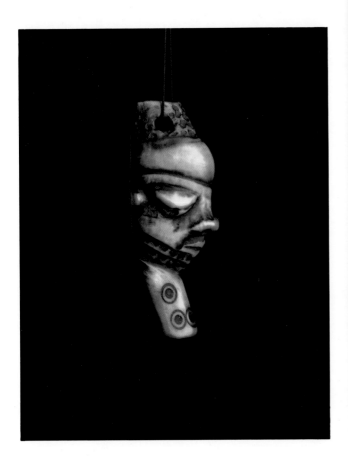

19. PENDE, Zaire / Pendant in the form of a mask, *ikhoko* / Ivory / H. 4.8 cm. (1⅞")

The Pende carve small ivory reproductions of several of their common mask types. These pendants, or *ikhoko*, are worn around the neck by those responsible for guarding masks from theft and destruction and by sick members of the community who hope to benefit from the healing power of the spirits the masks embody. A mask may "visit" a person who is ill and dance over the person's body. The magical power of the mask is then prolonged by wearing an *ikhoko* that represents it. The mask types that wear a long beard, including *phumbu, fumu,* and this *phota* mask, are considered especially effective in

curing the sick; these types are most frequently represented by carved ivory pendants.

The best ivory pendants were produced by the carvers of the Kisenzele clan in the village of Nioka-Kitamba, near Mukedi. Hippopotamus ivory was frequently used. Pendants were commonly worn by men, women, and children. Those carved of ivory were usually owned by men; women and children wore smaller, less elaborate *ikhoko* carved of wood or of the seed of the *muhafu* (*Canarium schweinfurti*) (de Sousberghe 1958: 73–74).

20. TSAAM (Tsaamba, Samba), Zaire / Drummer figure, *pindi* / Wood, split cane, animal hide / H. 26.7 cm. (10½")

The Tsaam were among the earliest Bantu-speaking immigrants to the area of central Zaire. After their arrival in the fifteenth century, they were scattered first by the Yaka, then by the Ngongo, Pindi, Suku, and Hungana, and finally by the Mbala. They have settled in widely scattered villages and small enclaves among larger populations. The Tsaam have produced numerous figures like this one that resemble the Mbala style and that have, as a result, been misattributed to the more numerous Mbala (Félix, pers. comm., 1988).

This figure was collected by Leo Frobenius on his first voyage to Zaire in 1905. It was acquired by the Hamburg Museum für Völkerkunde together with its female counterpart,

called *wenyi* or *gihalu giwenyi* (holding a child). Male figures were called *limba*. The drummer figures were part of the royal treasury and were used in enthronement ceremonies similar to those of the Tsaam's Mbala neighbors. A female figure holding a child, illustrated in Maes (1939: 188, ill. 63), appears to be by the same hand as this object.

Biebuyck says that the figures were called *pindi* and were kept carefully hidden. They were important to the royal treasury, and only the king could touch them without fear of death. The figures would be consulted before war, during judicial cases, or following bad harvests (Biebuyck 1985: 165).

21. CHOKWE, Zaire, Angola, Zambia / Mask / Vegetable fiber, wood / H. 24 cm. (9½")

Naturalistic animal masks were used by the Chokwe in performances associated with *mukanda* (initiation). The performer who wore this mask (and others like it now in the national museum in Zaire and the colonial museum in Lisbon) was said to dance on all fours, recreating the uncontrollable character of the bush pig. The mask was given the name *ngulu* (wild bush pig).

Among Bantu-speaking peoples the unpredictable and wild behavior of the bush pig is associated with females of all species, and the mask is said to reflect the difficulties men have controlling women. In hunters' societies, the symbolic hunt serves to illustrate and mediate tension between the sexes. This tension is reflected in the narrow line bifurcating this mask, which in many examples of this type is painted white.

22. CHOKWE, Angola / Mask / Wood, fiber / H. 29.3 cm. (11½")

This is the male counterpart, *chihongo*, of the female *mwana pwo* mask. Its type is recognized by the jutting beard and elaborate headgear. The distinctive features of the Chokwe style include the sunken orbits, the broad mouth, the filed teeth, and especially the graphic patterns, including the cross, *chingelyengelye*, on the forehead and the *masoji* (tear tracks) on the cheeks. These patterns are used on both male and female masks.

The *chihongo* represents the spirit of strength and wealth. It is worn by the chief or the son of the chief in ribald skits mimicking characters in the village. Such masks serve as agents of social control; in exchange for gifts from the members of the community, they bring about positive change by acting out the negative results of inaction.

23. KUBA, Zaire / Portrait of a king, *ndop* / Wood / H. 34.3 cm. (13½")

This is a portrait of Shyaam aMbul a Ngwoong, the most famous of the kings whose portraits were once preserved in Mushenge, the capital of the Kuba kingdom. The original portrait was removed to the British Museum in 1908 by Emil Torday. This figure was carved to replace the original between 1908 and 1916. It was made at the request of Kot Mabiintsh Ma-Kyeen, who presented it to Robert Reisdorf, King Leopold's personal envoy to the Kuba court between 1916 and 1929 (Félix, pers. comm.).

The figure was displayed in 1937 in Frans Olbrechts' famous exhibition of the art of Zaire, and is one of the few illustrated in the very rare original exhibition catalogue (Olbrechts 1937: no. 154). It is also illustrated in Olbrechts' *Les Arts plastiques du Congo belge* (1959) among a group of seventeen other portraits (middle row, fifth from left). It remained in Reisdorf's possession until his death, when it was sold by his heirs.

The subject of the portrait is identified by the game board attached to the plinth on which the figure is seated. Portraits such as this are called *ndop* and were carved beginning in the mid-eighteenth century, one figure to represent each king, until 1886, when a civil war disrupted the normal functioning of the court (Vansina 1978: 214). The reign of Shyaam began in about 1600 and marked the golden age of the Kuba. He was said to have been the son of a Bushoong slave who had traveled west to the kingdom of the Kongo, where he learned about the concept of centralized political authority and the design of an orderly city. It was during his reign that American crops, including corn, manioc, and peanuts, were introduced in Zaire, and ironworking, textile weaving, and woodcarving expanded dramatically (Rosenwald 1974: 28). He is also credited with the introduction of the board game *mankala* (Kuba *lyeel*), which became the symbol (*ibol*) of his reign. Emil Torday suggested that it was Shyaam himself who introduced the practice of carving these portraits.

This figure bears several emblems of Kuba kingship identical to those on the figure in the British Museum (see Adams 1988: 36). Among them are the wide belt of cowries, or *yeemy*, crossing the abdomen. Below it is a braided belt called *mwaandaan*. According to Joseph Cornet (1982) the *mwaandaan* can

never be untied; it represents the ability of the wearer to keep the secrets of the kingdom. The cowrie-covered bands on the biceps are called *mabiim*, the brass rings on the forearms *ntshyaang*. The ornaments over each shoulder are made of cane covered with cloth and are called *paang-angup* (hippopotamus teeth). Finally, all Kuba king figures wear the distinctive cap with its projecting bill (*shody*).

Scholars have speculated that the *ndop* figures collected early in this century may have been replacements for older objects carved during the reigns of the kings depicted. This theory, which would account for the marked stylistic similarities between many of the figures, is supported by the history of this object as a replacement for the figure now in the British Museum. Although this piece is clearly by a different hand than the older and significantly larger objects, it conforms strictly to convention in faithfully reproducing royal regalia.

24. BUSHOONG, Zaire / Mask, *Nyata a Masheke* / Wood, vegetable fiber, feathers / H. 65 cm. (25⅝")

The Bushoong, the ruling elite of the Kuba, live between the Kasai and Sankuru rivers. The Bushoong may have moved from the Atlantic coast to escape the slave trade; by the mid-seventeenth century, they were in the Kasai/Sankuru area, fighting the Bieeng for control of the region (Vansina 1960: 265). The Bushoong are only one of about eighteen subgroups that constitute the Kuba peoples. These include the "Maluk, Iding, Bokila, Ngoombe in the north; the Ngongo and Mbeengi in the east; the Bushong [*sic*], Bulaang, Pyaang and Ngende in the central and southern regions and the Kete and Bieeng in the southwest; the Ilebo, Shoowa, Kel, Kaam and Kayuweeng in the west. The Cwa (or Twa) Pygmies live scattered over the whole region" (Vansina 1960).

This large helmet mask, called *Nyata a Masheke*, was purchased from the former owner, Mikobi Ikeko, by Marc

Félix in the village of Mbamba Bishasha, where it was used in dances by the performer Bope Mikobi. The mask was "used at funerals of the highest-ranking members of society" (Félix, field notes, 1988). The mask shows evidence of much use; if in fact it appeared only for the funerals of very high-ranking people, such extensive use must indicate extreme age (Smith 1988).

In describing the funeral of an elderly Kuba woman, Torday notes the coating of the corpse with red camwood powder (*tukula*), burial in a palm-fiber coffin, and the distribution of small camwood-paste animal forms to the mourners (1925: 197). Recent research in the Kuba area by David Binckley and Patricia Darrish has shown the extensive use of masks at funerals of titleholders.

SOUTHERN SAVANNAH: Kasai / Sankuru Rivers Area

25. KUBA (Bushoong), Zaire / Cup / Wood, *tukula* / H. 18.5 cm. (7¼")

The Bushoong, led by their king, the *nyimi*, formed the Kuba ruling elite, administering through a system of clan councils and chiefs (Vansina 1960: 265–66). Royal status was displayed through elaborately decorated prestige items, such as cups.

This cup, used for drinking wine from the fermented sap of the raffia palm (*Raphia vinifera*), depicts a royal male. Traces still remain of the red cosmetic camwood powder, *tukula*, which was rubbed into such objects. The red powder contrasts with the copper color of the scarification patterns and other details. Since metal was reserved for the use of the *nyimi*, the use of copper indicates that this object belonged to royalty.

The cup shows the traditional flaring hairstyle of the Kuba, with triangular patterns shaved at the temples. The elongated head and the round scars on the cheekbones may indicate that the carver was Ndengese, working on a royal commission (Félix 1987: 28–29, 62–63). The exchange of prestige objects between the Kuba and the Ndengese is frequent and long-standing, for the Bushoong royal clan and the Ndengese are related.

Although Kuba cups are common in public and private collections, cups of this quality, with metal appliqué and much of the color preserved, are quite rare.

26. LELE (Bashilele, Leele), Zaire / Mask / Wood, pigment / H. 29 cm. (11⅜")

The Lele live west of the Kasai River, north of the Pende. The Kuba live just across the Kasai to the east. The Lele are believed to have come from the area of Lake Tumba and Lake Leopold II with the Kuba, crossing to the east of the Kasai only after clashes with the Bushoong (Douglas 1963: 110). They are a matrilineal society, organized around age grades. The largest political system is the village, which is nominally ruled by the village chief, the senior male of the founding clan, but is actually controlled by a balance of power between age sets (Douglas 1963: 68–77).

Lele masks are rare, and little is known about their function. Mary Douglas, who worked in the area in the 1950s, has said that the Lele do not make masks; but the style of this object conforms to conventions present in other objects, including boxes, pipes, and cups, that have been attributed to the Lele. These have been described in the entry for the beautiful Lele pipe in the Stanley Collection (no. 102 in the 1985 exhibition). Lele characteristics here include the very simple outline

of the mask, the arched eyes and brows, and the broad, flat planes of the cheeks. François Neyt attributes the mask to the Nguba area, near Djoko (Neyt 1981: 180).

It is not certain how the mask was used. It may have been worn in dances for the funerary rites of a chief (Neyt 1981: 180) or served as one of three masks used in annual reenactments of the founding of the Lele people (Félix 1987: 74). Masks are used in similar ways among the Kuba, who share a creation myth with the Lele. The spots on this mask also suggest the markings of a leopard, an animal of great importance among the Lele. When a man kills a leopard, he gains status in his age set. The skin of a leopard can be paid to the aristocratic clan of the Tundu as the fine for murder (Douglas 1963: 197). Diviners are said to transform themselves into leopards, especially when they battle the sorcerer of another village, who may also appear in the form of a leopard (Douglas 1963: 229).

27. BIOMBO, Zaire / Mask / Wood, pigment / H. 34 cm. (13⅜")

This mask shows the stylistic influence of several peoples on the Biombo, who live in a crossroads area between the Kuba and the southern Kete, the Eastern Pende, the Luluwa, and the Chokwe. The basic form is closest to the helmet masks of the Kuba and related peoples, especially the Kete, but the bright color and the use of geometric patterns, especially the alternating black and white triangles, are distinctive Pende style characteristics. Like the Pende, the Biombo have shared influences with the Chokwe, whose masks are noted for the curving brows linked above the nose and the deep, concave orbits around the eyes.

Such masks were used among all the peoples of the Kasai and Lulua rivers area in young men's initiations. There were three types of Biombo masks: the messenger *munginga*, of which this may be an example; the female *tshimoana* (nearly identical to the *munginga*); and the larger *muluala*, with protuberant conical eyes.

This mask was collected in southern Zaire in the first decade of this century by Leo Frobenius, and was in the collection of the Hamburg Museum für Völkerkunde. It was later in the Grannick Collection for many years until it was sold following Grannick's death.

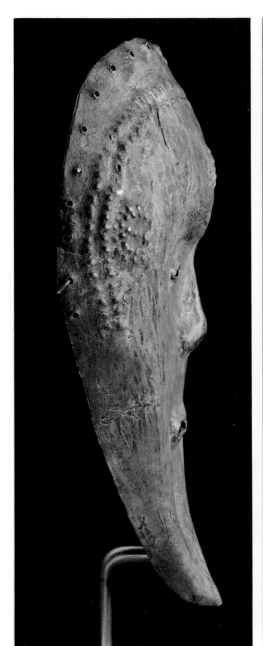

28. DING, Zaire and Angola / Mask / Copper / H. 32.2 cm. (12⅝")

The Ding, sometimes called the Kongo-Dinga, live on the west bank of the Kasai River where it flows from northern Angola into south-central Zaire. They are closely related to the Kongo, who live far to the west. To the north live the Kete and the Binji, and to the east the Lwalwa. The Ding often use wooden masks in the Lwalwa style, which they purchase from the Lwalwa or may carve themselves. The Lwalwa sometimes cover wooden masks in their own style with thin sheets of copper.

Sculpture of any kind is very rare in this area, and at this time there are only five copper Ding masks outside Africa. In the 1930s, a copper mask was photographed at night by a Portuguese anthropologist using the lights of his car. The first such mask to be taken out of Africa was collected in 1961 by Marie-Louise Bastin, who found it hidden in a tree in a Kongo village (Bastin 1961: 39).

This mask was made of copper using the repoussé technique, in which a malleable sheet of metal is hammered over a wooden form and patterns are pushed into the surface from the back to appear in low relief on the front of the mask. The mask was once covered with a thick layer of sacrificial material, which the African owner scraped away with a knife before the mask was sold, resulting in numerous scratches.

Ding copper masks represent Ngongo Munene, the Chief of the Earth, and are worn during the funeral of a chief, at the enthronement of his successor, at ceremonies honoring ancestors, and at boys' initiation camps. Since women and children were forbidden to see this mask, it was wrapped in cloth, stored in a gourd, and hidden in a small grass hut built in the fork of a tree.

29. EASTERN LUBA, Zaire / Head / Wood / H. 22.6 cm. (8½")

This object is one of the first examples of Luba or Luba-related art to reach Europe. It was brought to Belgium by members of the Society of African Missioners (the "White Fathers") in 1889–90 for an early exhibition of artifacts from what was then the Congo Free State.

The carved head has Luba stylistic elements, including a cascading coiffure associated with late-nineteenth-century central Luba, but resembles western Tabwa objects as well. It is very probable that this figure was collected near the Catholic mission at Mpala, an important Tabwa village on the southwestern shores of Lake Tanganyika. The White Fathers established a mission at Mpala in 1885, at the outpost of the International African Association founded by Emile Storms two years earlier. In the 1870s the Tabwa chiefs Kansabala and Lusinga moved to the vicinity of Mpala from lands along the Luvua River, adjacent to Eastern Luba peoples, whose villages they raided for the East African slave trade. Storms defeated the two chiefs in battle and seized from them important objects of Luba-style political regalia now in the collections of the Royal Museum of Central Africa, Tervuren (see Roberts and Maurer 1985). This figure is undoubtedly of similar origin, but was probably collected in 1888 or 1889 by Fathers Moncet and Moinet of Mpala Mission, who delivered fiery sermons against the evils of Tabwa religion and seized many pieces of sculpture. These were sent to the White Fathers' headquarters at Maison Carré in Algeria in late 1889, and were then distributed to Belgian and other churches for exhibition (White Fathers 1889–1900: entry of 9 Jan. 1889).

This object is probably of a genre called *kabwelulu*, central to the magico-religious practice of *bagabo*, a precolonial and early colonial secret society with members throughout what is now southeastern Zaire, reaching from the eastern Luba through the Hemba and Tabwa to the congeries of small ethnic groups living along the northwestern shores of Lake Tan-

ganyika. *Bagabo* protected its members from illness and other evil effects of sorcery by turning the force of a sorcerer's attack back upon the attacker (Vandergam 1930). Some of the magic devised by *bagabo* adepts is still in use today, such as powerful *mwanzambale* protective amulets; but other practices, such as those in which *kabwelulu* figures like this were used, have been abandoned. *Bagabo* was also a nativistic resistance movement with an explicitly antimissionary, anticolonial purpose—or so it was feared by resident Europeans. It can be assumed that the society helped its members to cope with their feelings of powerlessness in radically changing circumstances brought about by the imposition of a capitalist political economy by missionaries and Belgian colonizers.

A significant feature of this *kabwelulu* figure is the wide eyes that seem to stare into another dimension. According to an early description, a *bagabo* diviner would look deep into the eyes of his *kabwelulu* figure and then into the reflective surface of a pot of water, on which he had floated tiny wooden sculptures. He would "see" sorcerers "invisible" to those without his magical powers, accuse them, and force them to undergo the poison ordeal. In this way, evil was confronted and social harmony reestablished in the community (Van Vyve 1927).

Kabwelulu figures were attached to the tops of gourds (see no. 123 in the 1985 exhibition). Their bases were skirted with animal skins, and large snail shells and antelope horns filled with magical materials were often attached to or inserted in the gourd around the figure. This *kabwelulu* figure has a cavity in the top of the head that once held a potent magical bundle. The original surface, perhaps reddened with *nkula* powder from Pterocarpus bark, is glossy from polishing, possibly with European furniture wax by the White Fathers. The pronounced grain of the wood attests to the object's having been carved well over a century ago.

30. LUBA, Zaire' / Figure / Wood / H. 33 cm. (13")

This magnificent figure is a model for Luba body arts, and demonstrates the degree to which perfection of the body was considered a significant communicative social process for Luba people in late precolonial and early colonial times. The coiffure, for instance, is of the "cascade" style called *mabutu*, associated with turn-of-the-century central or east-central Luba (sometimes called Luba Shankadi). Mary Nooter (1991: 253, 412, 415) has reproduced a watercolor and a photograph rendered by W. F. P. Burton in the 1920s in which both the aesthetic sophistication of such a hairdo and the difficulty of creating and maintaining it are apparent. The lower register of the coiffure was built around a support, secured by long iron pins, and set off with beads and buttons. The central knot above the center of the woman's forehead was adorned with beads, emphasizing the line of scarification leading down the center of the forehead.

On the Stanley figure, a line of scarification leads from the ears to the line of the eyes, with an implied junction with the perpendicular line down the center of the forehead. Such a scarification pattern was practiced by other peoples of what is now southeastern Zaire, including the Tabwa, who call it "face of the cross" and still use it to emphasize the point between the eyes that is the seat of prophetic wisdom (Roberts 1990b: 11–12). The figure's chest and abdomen are also richly decorated with scarification in patterns with names that make poetic or ironic allusions to Luba life (M. Nooter 1991: 246). Among the Hemba (Luba-influenced peoples to the northeast of the Luba heartland), a male sculptor of ancestral figures would trace patterns and make incisions on a young woman's "less intimate parts of the body, leaving the rest to a woman" to complete (Kazadi Ntole 1980: 2–3). Different parts of the body were scarified as a girl matured, with the most painful operations performed last. Although some scarification patterns are no longer created, others are still used as important statements of female being.

The pain endured, as well as the increasing communication of erotic beauty, led to the cultural transformation from girl to woman (Roberts 1988a). So, too, did elongation of the labia majora, also seen on this figure. "Elder Luba women insist on the importance of this attribute assuring a woman's sense of dignity" and erotic pleasure (M. Nooter 1991: 249). Names given to such a perfected state, or lack thereof, also indicate that this body art further represents the achievement of a state consistent with cultural refinement as defined in Luba cosmogonic myths (de Heusch 1972: 33–35; cf. Roberts 1986: 22–23).

In their communicative capacity these various body arts were similar to graphic forms (wall and rock paintings or the studding with beads and carved images of *lukasa*, "memory boards") and to significant phenomena recognized or created in nature such as constellations of stars and trail blazes chipped on trees by Luba and other peoples of southeastern Zaire (Roberts 1988a; M. Nooter 1990: 40–41). Such expression offered "visual support for a certain vision of the world" (Kazadi Ntole 1980: 9) that was important to Luba religion and political economy, and, indeed, can be called a "tegumentary language" (Zahan 1975: 101). It is quite possible, for instance, that the Stanley figure is an example of the *masubu* figures displayed during the last phases of initiation to *budye*, a secret society that both reinforced the ideology of Luba sacred rule and was a counterweight to it (M. Nooter 1990: 40). As such, it would stand in explicit reference to tutelary and ancestral spirits of the society but would provide a general visual statement of royal bearing and being, a statement based on the ultimate social values embodied by the perfected Luba woman-lover-mother. One can only imagine the impact of such a beautifully achieved object as it was revealed in the dramatic processes of Budye initiation.

31. LUBA, Zaire / Pendant female torso / Ivory / H. 8.9 cm. (3½") **32. SONGYE, Zaire / Mask, *kifwebe* / Wood / H. 33 cm. (13")**

This tiny figure is carved from the tusk of a bush pig or a hippopotamus. The rich, translucent orange-red patina is the result of the application of palm oil, and the features have been softened by years of being worn on a cord strung over one shoulder across the body, suspended beneath an arm. This example bears the circle-and-dot motif that is ubiquitous on ivories everywhere in the world, from the Arctic Circle to the grasslands and forests of Zaire.

Although Joseph Cornet (1972: 220) states that such objects remind the wearer of a deceased relative, it is more likely that they represent *vidye*, spirits of nature and the wilderness, and are intended to protect the wearer from disasters of all kinds. All are pierced transversely behind the breasts for suspension.

According to Dunja Hersak (1986), this fine old Songye mask, called *kifwebe* (pl. *bifwebe*), may be distinguished as a female mask by its white color and the flat crest from the front to the back of the head. The term *kifwebe* describes the mask, the mask society, and the wearer of the mask, who, in a trancelike state (*bwadi*), becomes neither person nor spirit but *kifwebe* (Merriam 1974: 144).

The secret male mask society (*bwadi bwa kifwebe*) first appeared among the Songye soon after the turn of the century and had generally disbanded by the 1920s, although remnants still remain among the Eastern Songye. The society seems to have developed as a means of dealing with increasing competition for political power by controlling rival political factions through sorcery:

The masqueraders inflict punitive ills upon the populace and absolve them through payment, thus increasing the resources of chiefs and elders who are the anonymous and ruling members of the *bwadi bwa kifwebe* society. At the same time, rivals of the political elite may be subjugated by involuntary initiation into the *kifwebe* society of sorcerers. (Hersak 1986: 168)

A very similar mask, perhaps by the same hand, is illustrated in the catalogue of the Tishman Collection (Vogel 1981: 218).

33. BEMBE, Zaire / Figure / Wood / H. 71.5 cm. (28⅜")

The Bembe live west of Lake Tanganyika, southeast of the Lega and north of the Tabwa. Their neighbors to the southwest are the Boyo. Like all of their neighbors to the west, Bembe families, or clans, carved figures of ancestors. This piece was carved by the Basi Kasingo clan, whose members live in both Bembe and Boyo communities. A few even live in Lega villages. The Basi Kasingo are not an ethnic group or tribe (Félix, pers. comm.). They live in an area of high mountainous forests and grasslands, dissected by large rivers that flow east toward the lake.

The Bembe are best known for spectacular helmet masks with four huge eye sockets painted red and white, and similar small figures with concave faces, used by the *elanda* associa-tion. The tradition of carving large ancestral figures is linked to their western neighbors, such as the Hemba, Boyo, Bangu-bangu, and Kusu, and to the Tabwa to the south. Each of these peoples is represented in the Stanley Collection, and the figures of most share the upright columnar pose, arms parallel to the sides, narrowed torso (to allow for space between the arms and torso), angular legs, and the large spherical head we see in this example.

The triangular face, the enormous convex, almond-shaped eyes, the small protuberant mouth, and the broad, flat nose are characteristics that this object shares with others carved for the Basi Kasingo clan.

34. TABWA, Zaire / Figure / Wood / H. 29 cm. (11½")

This figure, collected in Africa by Marc Félix in the mid-1970s, is remarkably similar to five others in two private Belgian collections (illustrated in Roberts and Maurer 1985: 142–44). Four of these were collected as a set near the town of Moba, in east-central Tabwa territory. All six figures have the same proportions, with exaggerated necks and torsos; all have short arms and stubby fingers that touch the abdomen below the ribs and point toward their prominent navels; and all six have the same facial composition, featuring wide eyes and mouths. Like this figure, three of the others have long, pendant coiffures and are probably male; the two others have closer chignons and may be female. Each has some variation of the facial and body scarification seen here. The similarity of the six figures suggests that they were produced in a single workshop, or, at the very least, were made to reflect a common, closely defined aesthetic.

The Stanley figure exhibits a language of body arts that can be "read" (Roberts 1988a). The hairdo, for instance, is called *buyange*, a term associated with a hunting cult that the Tabwa shared with the Luba and Lunda peoples to the west. The preparation of a *buyange* coiffure was a long process, demanding a great deal of patience. Strands of hair were bound with strips of locally produced bark cloth, thickly coated with castor oil and crimson camwood powder, and braided in several different patterns similar to those used in mat weaving and basketry.

The isosceles triangles of the lower portion of this figure's coiffure are a motif called *balamwezi*, "the rising of a new moon," that is an allusion to one of the most significant metaphors of Tabwa philosophy. Tabwa recognize an association between moonlight and enlightenment, and the appearance of a new moon each month is a time of celebration, signifying

the triumph of wisdom over ignorance, good over evil, and courage over fear (Roberts 1985b: 1–3).

The hairdo is also divided down the middle in a line echoing short segments of scarification on the figure's forehead and on the abdomen just above the navel. These follow the human body midline, poetically called *mulalambo*, or "where the buffalo sleeps." *Mulalambo* refers to watersheds, the horizon line of Lake Tanganyika, the Milky Way, and other lines of demarcation that define symmetry and balance. Scarification of this sort perfects the body, establishing a metaphorical, harmonious relationship between the cosmos and the individual's physical and social being (Roberts 1988a: 48).

Like the figures it resembles, this one has badly eroded legs and feet, suggesting that the figures were either stuck in the ground or placed in a shrine where they fell victim to termites and water damage. The eye shape of the six figures suggests

possible uses they may have served. Three of the other five have wide, lozenge-shaped eyes like the Stanley figure, and probably represent the ancestors (*mipasi*) of chiefs and other lineage elders. The other two have oddly peaked, diamond-shaped eyes, which the Tabwa used to represent the prescient stare of those whose powerful magic allows them to see beyond the ken of ordinary people. They probably portray renowned healers and magical practitioners. Such figures were and still are used in curing.

According to an anonymous turn-of-the-century Tabwa catechist, the ancestors provide prophetic dreams and other guidance that "brightens or brings light to someone's eyes" (*mipasi yobe ikuswezizwe pa menso*), allowing that person the extraordinary powers necessary to counteract the forces of evil (cited in Roberts 1985a: 12, 41).

35. TABWA, Zaire and Zambia / Beaded mask / Glass beads, leather, rooster feathers, monkey pelts / H. 88.9 cm. (35")

This mask was collected in the mid-1970s by Marc Félix near the northern end of Lake Mweru, where the Luba, Tabwa, eastern Lunda, and Bemba cultural spheres converge. The mask may be associated with *mbudye*, a secret society that celebrates the mythical charter and values of Luba royalty (M. Nooter 1990). More specifically, its iconography is an elaboration of the simpler beaded headdresses worn by diviners of the *bulumbu* possession cult found among the Tabwa and the Eastern Luba. Such headdresses are called *nyaka*, or pangolin, from a metaphorical association between the beaded triangles and the similarly shaped scales of that animal. Like this mask, *bulumbu* headdresses are often surmounted by feathers and have animal pelts attached to the top that cover the wearer's head and hang down his or her back (Roberts 1988b; 1990a).

The white spiral at the center of the forehead represents the "eye" of Kibawa, an earth spirit that the Eastern Luba associate with the culture hero Mbidi Kiluwe and that the Tabwa feel is the keeper of their dead. Kibawa's cavern is near the Luvua River in the general area where this mask was collected, and was visited by Luba and Tabwa as an oracle early in this century. The Tabwa now feel that Kibawa sends forth the spirits that possess *bulumbu* adepts during séances that are convened to seek explanations and cures for illness and other misfortunes. The center of the forehead covered by the beaded spiral is felt to be the locus of wisdom and prophetic vision.

The spiral eye of Kibawa also represents the moon. The event of possession by a spirit issuing from the depths of

Kibawa's cavern is called "the rising of a new moon," the name Tabwa also give to the triangular motif so important to their art (also used in the coiffure of the Tabwa ancestral figure, no. 34). The new moon and other symbols reflect a message of enlightenment, courage, and the dawning of hope after a period of "obscurity." The rooster feathers along the top of the mask refer to the beginning of the new day (marked by a rooster crowing) and so, figuratively, to a life endowed with new insight. In a related manner, the white chalk with which *bulumbu* adepts cover their faces is "moonlight," which conveys a sense of purity and receptivity as well as enlightened vision (Roberts 1990b).

The isosceles triangles on either side of the spiral are the "doors" of possessing spirits that emanate from Kibawa's cavern; other triangles echo these and repeat the "rising of the new moon" motif. The choice of bead colors (especially those outside the Tabwa primary triad of white, red, and black) is determined by availability and aesthetics rather than esoteric symbolism. The pelts attached to the mask are of the arboreal blue monkey (*Cercopithecus mitis*); it is hoped that a *bulumbu* spirit will "mount" the person and possess him or her, just as the blue monkey occupies the highest branches of a tree. This idea is dramatized in dance, as the field photographs of Marc Félix show; with every leap of the masked dancer, the blue monkey pelts seem to rise up and then settle back down, reestablishing their ascendancy atop the dancer's head.

36. TABWA, Zaire and Zambia / Buffalo mask / Wood / H. 73.7 cm. (29")

What does a Tabwa person "become" when he dons a buffalo mask? Several traits of buffalo anatomy and behavior are significant by Tabwa reckoning. Buffaloes are found in herds in which reddish cows and black bulls live together in the light forests of Tabwa country. Ordinarily as docile as cattle, they are notoriously dangerous when disturbed or wounded. Buffaloes are mostly crepuscular (most active at dusk and dawn); although enormous, they are virtually able to disappear into thickets during the daytime. Buffaloes are also fond of mud wallows, in which they may submerge themselves almost completely, and they seem to swim in rivers and lakes for the pleasure of it. The Tabwa fear of buffaloes is due in large part to the animals' apparent invisibility; buffaloes are there but not seen, and are thus doubly menacing.

Buffaloes, then, possess paradoxically opposite traits: they are red and black, docile and aggressive, visible and invisible, in water and out, and active at the thresholds of dusk and dawn. They present a divided or dichotomous nature; this suggests to the Tabwa a metaphorical bridge between buffaloes and humans. In particular, buffaloes are associated with chiefs and culture heroes for the Tabwa and related peoples of southern Zaire. Chiefs and culture heroes are oddly divided beings; as "fathers of their people," they are seen as sources of wisdom, nurturance, and protection, but they are also feared as the most heinous sorcerers of the land. For the Tabwa this belief explains the deadly dialectic of greed among the most benevolent of men. Culture heroes are half-beings divided down the middle, thus embodying the ambiguous nature of authority (Roberts, in press). The paradoxes of social life are further reflected in the Tabwa practice of scarification along the human body midline, a line called *mulalambo*, or "where the buffalo sleeps" (see no. 34).

Tabwa buffalo masks may be called *kiyunde*, and they may have been worn in dances together with female face or helmet masks called *musangwe* (Roberts 1990a). *Kiyunde* may refer to healing and the smelting of iron, activities associated with Tabwa culture heroes. *Musangwe* is from a Tabwa verb meaning "to be found," or "to desire," which suggests both sexual promiscuity and the magical quality of finding or achieving what one desires through the guidance of ancestral spirits. Perhaps the buffalo and female masks were worn together to dramatize origin myths in which culture heroes established both the order and the ambiguities of human life.

EAST AFRICA

37. KARAGWE, Tanzania / Buffalo / Iron / H. 19 cm. (7½")

This forged iron figure of a buffalo was once part of the royal treasury of the kingdom of Karagwe, just west of Lake Victoria. James Hanning Speke saw iron objects in 1861, and Henry Morton Stanley saw ten iron figures in 1876 in the court of King Rumanika at Bweranyange (Speke 1863; Stanley 1890). The oral tradition of the court indicated that they had been forged by Rumanika's father, Ndagara. It is doubtful that they were made by the king himself, who belonged to a clan of herders who disdained manual labor; they were probably made by the Basindi clan of smiths. Alternatively, the figures may have been brought from Bunyoro at the end of the sixteenth or

the beginning of the seventeenth century by Ruhinda, the founder of the kingdom (Bruyninx 1983; 1988: 311).

The royal herds held extraordinary importance for the pastoral Karagwe. This object may have incorporated some magical power over the well-being of the herds of the Karagwe kingdom (Sassoon 1983).

Three similar figures are in the collection of the Linden Museum in Stuttgart, given to the museum in 1906 by a Dr. Feldmann. Two others are in Belgian private collections (Bruyninx 1988).

38. NYAMWEZI, Tanzania / Figure / Wood / H. 67.3 cm. (26½")

Little is known about this figure from the Nyamwezi, owing in part to the paucity of art history research in East Africa to date and in part to the nature of the Nyamwezi themselves. "Nyam-wezi" is a name given by outsiders to a loose congeries of peoples in central Tanzania, meaning "people of the moon." Among these people "there is little, if any, feeling of unity as a tribe. . . . There is no common myth of tribal origin, and no customs or institutions which are common to them but peculiar to them" (A. D. Roberts 1973: 117). The first to define the Nyamwezi in this way were coastal peoples to their east, with whom Nyamwezi came into contact as caravan trade to and across what is now central Tanzania intensified during the nineteenth century. Swahili traders from the coast, in their quest for slaves and ivory from the heart of central Africa (now Zaire), settled among Nyamwezi at what is now the important town of Tabora. Several Nyamwezi chiefs were able to take advantage of such a situation by consolidating their own powers and prerogatives. As their power increased, Nyamwezi became middlemen in the coastal trade and sent their own expeditions, often as mercenaries accompanying Swahili traders, to raid and settle among central African peoples such as the Tabwa, who live southwest of Lake Tanganyika.

It can be assumed that one expressive vehicle for such a consolidation and extension of power was the creation of what may be termed "statement art," of which the Hehe stool, or "throne" (no. 42), is an excellent example. Nyamwezi chiefs are also known to have possessed high-backed stools or thrones, such as a magnificent example now in the Museum für Völkerkunde in Berlin (Roberts and Maurer 1985: 186–87; first discussed in Luschan 1900). The head and face of the Stanley figure are of a similar style, with inset white beads for eyes (one here being lost) that may refer to extended vision through a lunar metaphor. This figure and others like it might have played an auxiliary role, either ritual or spiritual, to the thrones.

As in the Hehe throne, an ancestral or spirit figure is incorporated into the Berlin throne in such a way that it "embraces" the person who (at least figuratively) is entitled to sit on it. The backs of both of these thrones are also the backs, chests, and torsos of the figures. The planklike body of the Nyamwezi figure illustrated here may have been meant to refer directly to a throne as the "seat" of ancestral/divine and secular powers, as a further or corroborative statement of the sacred authority that the throne represented. That the figure is female reinforces this hypothesis, for Nyamwezi-related peoples call their mothers' agnatic kin "the back," recalling the way that children are carried in early infancy (Shorter 1972: 68–69). It can be assumed, then, that the figure is meant to suggest an association between a chief's rule and the security and nurturing of one's mother and her kin. The lack of feet and the patina on the lower legs of the figure suggest that it was set into something else, perhaps an earthen shrine.

39. KWERE, ZARAMO, and other matrilineal peoples, Tanzania / Figures / Wood / H. 10–20 cm. (4–8")

Most of the matrilineal peoples of eastern Tanzania produce small, stylized figures like these to be used by female initiates during the period of seclusion that accompanies puberty and the ceremonies associated with rejoining the community. The same shapes are used on other types of objects, including chairs, staffs, musical instruments, and snuff containers made by each of these peoples. The major styles represented by this small group of objects are those of the Zaramo and the Kwere. The Zaramo carve a sagittal crest with flanking hemispheres to represent the hairstyle; the neighboring Kwere use the same conventions, but the crest is usually bifurcated and flares outward. Zaramo figures rarely include facial features; Kwere figures often do.

Over the past thirty years several scholars have studied the initiations in which these figures appear (Swantz 1970). Most recently Marc Félix has published the results of his research during a period when he was actively collecting a large number of these objects, including the present examples. He writes:

The puberty rites began at the onset of menstruation, and were devised to help the female child (*mwali*) become a responsible, mature woman who would take her place in society as a good wife and mother. . . . A girl's aunt (*shangazi*), her father's eldest sister, was an important person in her life, and would be present at her birth. . . . At puberty the aunt was again present, bringing with her the family heirlooms: a chain necklace made of iron and a little doll-like figure made of wood (*mwana nya nghiti*, "child of wood," "tree," or "chair"). . . . The figurine was tied on a cord around the young initiate's neck, or hung at the foot of her bed. (Félix 1990: 173–75)

The *shangazi* told the young initiate about the prohibitions that the members of her family must observe and the importance of the wooden carvings that helped to perpetuate life forces. "The stated purpose of this seclusion was to fatten the initiate to enhance her eventual fertility, to lighten her complexion, to teach her submission, and to prevent any sexual contact with males" (Félix 1990: 176).

40. PARE, KWERE, Tanzania / Figures / Wood, cloth / H. 10–15 cm. (4–6")

Among the matrilineal peoples of coastal Tanzania, figures like these were used in a number of contexts by many different groups. Human figures, often with bits of cloth or hair attached, commemorated deceased relatives and were owned by members of the deceased's own clan. According to Marc Félix (1990), some of the larger figures contain cavities into which relics of the ancestors were placed. Animal figures represented spirits of the wilderness and were used as sources of magical power by diviners, healers, and hunters.

Among the most interesting of these are the Pare figure of an elephant, perhaps used by a hunter, and the figure with one red eye and one leg, which in its lack of balance must have been a source of potent power for a diviner.

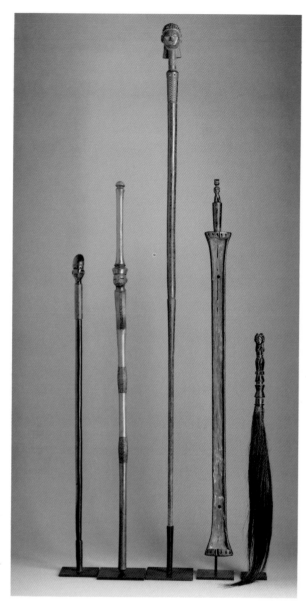

41. ZARAMO, KWERE, MAKONDE, Tanzania / Staffs, harp, fly whisk / Wood / H. 83.8–73.7 cm. (33–29")

Throughout Africa, staffs and related fly whisks represent authority and status. Among the matrilineal peoples of eastern Tanzania, staffs were carried as symbols of status by male heads of villages, female heads of lineages, healers, diviners, and many others. The *mwana hiti* figures used in Tanzania are important for the continuity and welfare of the clan; they appear on virtually all status objects, including musical instruments. Marc Félix has described staffs that bear *mwana hiti* figures:

Mwana hiti was so much a part of life for the Zaramo and the Kwere that it had a role to play even before they were conceived. A diviner, who could be male or female, would be consulted when a woman had difficulty conceiving. The diviner's staff was usually surmounted

with a *mwana hiti*, or sometimes topped with a more naturalistic human figuration. This staff was a status symbol, part of the regalia, but also an implement. When consulted by a barren woman, to discover the cause of her misfortune the diviner used this staff to make symbolic drawings in the sand. (Félix 1990: 159)

Staffs were also used in the context of initiation:

On the morning of the eighth day of the initiation the *wasepi* carried the boy piggyback into the forest for a procession in which only initiated men could participate. It was led by *mpengo*, who was carrying an initiation staff or pole that depicted the piggyback icon. Gourds containing symbolic ingredients might be hanging from this staff. (Félix 1990: 167)

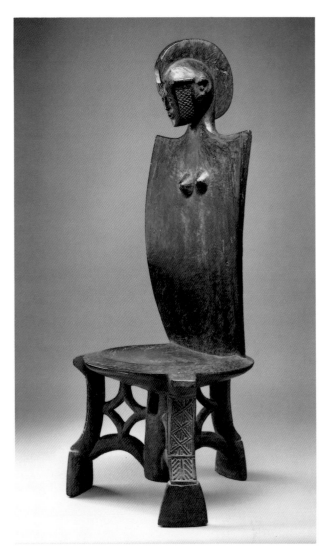

42. HEHE or LUGURU, Tanzania / Stool or "throne" / Wood / H. 91.5 cm. (36")

Hehe peoples are still known for the bellicosity they exhibited in the late nineteenth and early twentieth centuries; indeed, "Hehe" is a sobriquet given to them by their adversaries, who heard, all too often by their reckoning, the war cry of "Hey, hey, hey, we are fighting the enemy, e-hey!" (Redmayne 1973: 38). Those now called Hehe lived in much smaller groups until the mid-nineteenth century, when their growing participation in the intense activity of Swahili slave and ivory traders from Zanzibar and the East African coast swept them into a wider political economy. Hehe chiefs consolidated their powers to take advantage of new opportunities for trade and warfare, both to capture slaves, cattle, and ivory and to defend against the predations of rivals, especially the dreaded Ngoni to their southwest and the Masai to the north. By the 1890s, several Hehe chiefs were so well organized militarily that they could thwart German conquest of what was to become Tanganyika Territory. Not until the very end of the century did the Germans defeat the Hehe through attrition; by this time the Hehe had won German respect, to the point of being called the "master race" of East Africa. As Alison Redmayne has noted, "This [history] has had an effect on the way Europeans

and other Africans have regarded the Hehe ever since" (1973: 42–55).

This magnificent Hehe "throne" must be understood in this context. In all probability, a Hehe chief or other important person commissioned it as an object of "statement art" to serve "the glorification or reinforcement of existing systems of authority" (McLeod 1976: 99). The creation of statement art is a conscious strategy for explaining, justifying, and celebrating newfound authority through the cooptation of older symbols of power, the generation of new ones, or the borrowing of cogent metaphors from esteemed neighbors. Rulers seeking to consolidate their power invented "traditions" in this way (Roberts 1985b: 10–16).

The high-backed stool or "throne" was an idiom of statement art extending from the East African coast westward across Tanzania to southeastern Zaire and northeastern Zambia (N. Nooter 1989). In 1900, Felix von Luschan first drew attention to formal similarities between Nyamwezi and Tabwa thrones in the collections of the Museum für Völkerkunde in Berlin; he also suggested that the idea of a high-backed stool probably originated locally and was not modeled after European chairs. A map by Marc Félix (1990: 152–53, 495–96) illustrates the stylistic modification of the throne's basic idea, moving from the Zaramo, Doe, and Kwere peoples on the coast just north of Dar es Salaam through the Gogo, Luguru, Hehe, Kimbu, and Nyamwezi of central Tanzania to the Tabwa, Bemba, and Lungu along the southwestern shores of Lake Tanganyika. The idea of the throne was modified by each group to suit local aesthetics and metaphors of sacred power.

This piece shows striking similarity to several other thrones that have been collected recently near the important trade towns of Morogoro and Dodoma among the Luguru and Gogo peoples (including a superb example now at the National Museum of African Art in Washington, D.C.), and may be one of a pair; for the other, see Leurquin and Meurant 1990: 16–17, fig. 5. Since no specific information is available indicating who made or used any of these pieces, the loose term "Hehe" must suffice to refer to the general culture area of their origin.

The functional double-entendre of this throne is obvious, for the back of the stool is also the back and torso of the figure; by extension, the seat and legs of the stool also make anatomical reference (cf. Leurquin and Meurant 1990: 18). The effect,

seen in other East African thrones, is to embrace the person who sits on the stool. Since it is unlikely that anyone could or would sit on this stool or others like it (notably two Tabwa examples illustrated in Roberts and Maurer 1985: 184, 277), their purpose seems entirely figurative: to represent the "seat" of sacred power embraced by an ancestral or spiritual presence (Roberts 1985b: 16). The crested coiffure and the scarification on the face, echoed in the geometrical designs on the back and legs of the stool (also scarification?), were popular Hehe women's body arts in the late nineteenth century; both serve as broader ideological metaphors of female nurturing, dependency, and protection with which a powerful chief would want to be associated.

Two features of the Stanley throne remain enigmatic. First, although the carved breasts and body arts suggest a female presence, the figure also has an Adam's apple, suggesting male, androgynous, or more generally dualistic principles. Second, the central, rounded structure of the undercarriage is hollowed out, which may suggest some practical purpose (mounting or carrying the throne on a pole?).

SELECTED BIBLIOGRAPHY
INDEX

SELECTED BIBLIOGRAPHY

Adams, Monni
 1988 "18th-Century Kuba King Figures," *African Arts* 21(3): 32–38, 88.
Adelman, Kenneth Lee
 1975 "The Art of the Yaka," *African Arts* 9(1): 42.
Amon d'Aby, F. J.
 1960 *Croyances religieuses et coutumes juridiques des Agni de Côte d'Ivoire*. Paris: Larose.
Andersson, Efraim
 1953 *Contribution à l'ethnographie des Kuta*. Vol. 1. Studia Ethnographica Upsaliensa 6. Uppsala: Almqvist and Wiksell.
Bassani, Ezio
 1977–78 "Una bottega di grandi artisti bambara," *Critica d'Arte* 42(154–156): 209–228; 43(160–162): 181–200.
Bastin, Marie-Louise
 1961 "Un masque en cuivre martelé des Kongo du nord et de l'Angola," *Africa-Tervuren* 7.
 1982a *La Sculpture tshokwe*. Meudon: Alain and Françoise Chaffin.
 1982b *Sculptures angolaises*. Arnouville: Arts d'Afrique Noire.
 1984a *Introduction aux arts d'Afrique Noire*. Brussels: Presses Universitaires de Bruxelles.
 1984b Personal communication.
Beier, Ulli
 1957 *The Story of Sacred Wood Carvings from One Small Yoruba Town*. Lagos: Nigeria Magazine.
Ben Amos, Paula
 1980 *The Art of Benin*. London: Thames and Hudson.
Biebuyck, Daniel
 1972 "Bembe Art," *African Arts* 5(3): 12–19, 75–84.
 1973 *Lega Culture: Art, Initiation, and Moral Philosophy among a Central African People*. Berkeley, Los Angeles: University of California Press.
 1976a "Sculpture from the Eastern Zaire Forest Regions," *African Arts* 9(2): 8–15, 79.
 1976b "Sculpture from the Eastern Zaire Forest Regions: Mbole, Yela, and Pere." *African Arts* 10(1): 54–61, 99–100.
 1977 "Sculpture from the Eastern Zaire Forest Regions: Metoko, Lengola, and Komo," *African Arts* 10(2): 52–58.
 1981 *Statuary from the pre-Bembe Hunters*. Tervuren: Royal Museum of Central Africa.
 1984 Personal communication.
 1985 *The Arts of Zaire*, vol. 1. *Southwestern Zaire*. Berkeley and Los Angeles: University of California Press.
 1986 *The Arts of Zaire*, vol. 2. *Eastern Zaire: The Ritual and Artistic Context of Voluntary Associations*. Berkeley and Los Angeles: University of California Press.
Bogaerts, H.
 1950 "Bij de Basala Mpasu," *Zaire* 4(4): 379–419.
Boone, Olga
 1961 *Carte ethnique du Congo: Quart sud-est*. Tervuren: Musée Royal de l'Afrique Centrale.
 1973 *Carte ethnique de la République du Zaire*. Tervuren: Musée Royal de l'Afrique Centrale.

Bourgeois, Arthur P.
 1980 "Yaka Masks and Sexual Imagery." Unpublished paper presented at the 23rd annual meeting of the African Studies Association as part of the panel Eroticism in the African Arts.
 1981 "Kakungu Among the Yaka and Suku," *African Arts* 14(1): 42–46, 88.
 1984a *Art of the Yaka and Suku*. Meudon: Alain and Françoise Chaffin.
 1984b Personal communication.
Brousse
 1958 "La Fonction de la sculpture traditionelle chez les Ngbaka," *Brousse II*. Leopoldville: Courrier d'Afrique.
Bruyninx, E.
 1983 "Enkele merkwaardige ijzerplastieken uit N. W.-Tanzania," in *Liber memorialis Prof. Dr. P. J. Vandenhoute 1913–1978*, ed. Herman Burssens, E. Bruyninx, and R. Haeserijn. Gent: Rijksuniversiteit Gent.
 1988 *Utotombo: L'Art d'Afrique noire dans les collections privées belges*. Brussels: Société des Expositions du Palais des Beaux Arts.
Burssens, Hermann
 1962 "Yanda-beelden en Mani-sekte bij de Azande," *Annales du Musée Royal de l'Afrique Centrale*, Sciences humaines, Nouvelle série 4(4).
Burton, W. F. P.
 1961 *Luba Religion and Magic in Custom and Belief*. Tervuren: Musée Royal de l'Afrique Centrale, Série Sciences Humaines 35.
Cameron, Verney Lovett
 1877 *Across Africa*. London.
Carroll, L. Kevin
 1984 Personal communication.
Casati, Gaetano
 1891 *Ten Years in Equitoria and the Return with Emin Pasha*. 2 vols. London: Frederick Warne.
Claerhout, A.
 1984 *Ancient Terracotta Statuary and Pottery from Djenne, Mali*. Antwerp: Dessers.
Colle, P.
 1913 *Les Baluba*. Brussels: Collection de Monographies Ethnographiques 10, 11.
Cornet, Joseph
 1971 *Art of Africa: Treasures from the Congo*. New York: Phaidon.
 1972 *Art de l'Afrique noire au pays du Fleuve Zaire*. Brussels: Arcade.
 1978 *A Survey of Zairian Art: The Bronson Collection*. Raleigh: North Carolina Museum of Art.
 1982 *Art royal kuba*. Milan: Sipiel.
DeMott, Barbara
 1982 *Dogon Masks: A Structural Study of Form and Meaning*. Ann Arbor: UMI Research Press.
 1984 Personal communication.
Devisch, Renaat
 1972 "Signification socio-culturelle des masques chez les Yaka," *Instituto de Investigaçao Cientifica de Angola. Bolletim* 9(2): 151–176.

Dias, A. Jorge
    1961   *Portuguese Contribution to Cultural Anthropology.* Johannesburg: Witwatersrand University Press.

Dias, A. Jorge and Margot Dias
    1964   *Os Macondes de Moçambique, vol. 2: Cultura Material.* Lisbon: Junta de Investigaçoes do Ultramar.
    1970   *Os Macondes de Moçambique, vol. 3: Vida Social e Ritual.* Lisbon: Junta de Investigaçoes do Ultramar.

Dieterlen, Germaine
    1984   Personal communication.

Douglas, Mary
    1957   "Animals in Lele Religious Symbolism," *Africa* 27(1): 46–58.
    1963   *The Lele of the Kasai.* London: The International African Institute.

Drewal, Henry
    1980   *African Artistry: Technique and Aesthetics in Yoruba Sculpture.* Atlanta: The High Museum of Art.
    1983   "Art and Divination Among the Yoruba: Composition, Myth, and Motif," paper presented at the 26th African Studies Association meeting, Boston.
    1984   Personal communication.

Drewal, Henry John and Margaret Thompson Drewal
    1983   *Gelede: Art and Female Power Among the Yoruba.* Bloomington: Indiana University Press.

Ezra, Kate
    1984   Personal communication.

Fagg, William B.
    1970   *African Sculpture.* New York: The International Exhibitions Foundation.
    1980   *Masques d'Afrique.* Geneva: Nathan.

Fagg, William and John Pemberton
    1982   *Yoruba Sculpture of West Africa.* New York: Knopf.

Fagg, William B. and Margaret Plass
    1964   *African Sculpture: An Anthology.* London: Studio Vista.

Félix, Marc Leo
    1987   *100 Peoples of Zaire and Their Sculpture.* Brussels: Tribal Arts Press.
    1988   Field notes, personal communication.
    1989   *Maniema: An Essay on the Distribution of the Symbols and Myths as Depicted in the Masks of Greater Maniema.* Munich: Galerie Fred Jahn.
    1990   *Mwana Hiti: Life and Art of the Matrilineal Bantu of Tanzania.* Munich: Galerie Fred Jahn.

Fernandez, James W. and Renate L. Fernandez
    1975   "Fang Reliquary Art: Its Quantities and Qualities," *Cahiers d'Etudes Africaines* 15(4): 723–746.

Fischer, Eberhard and Hans Himmelheber
    1984   *The Arts of the Dan in West Africa.* Zurich: Museum Rietberg.

Flam, Jack D.
    1970   "The Symbolic Structure of Baluba Caryatid Stools," *African Arts* 4(2): 54–59.

Geary, Christraud
    1983   *Things of the Palace.* Wiesbaden: Franz Steiner Verlag.

Glaze, Anita
    1981   *Art and Death in a Senufo Village.* Bloomington: Indiana University Press.

Gohring, Heinz
    1970   *Baluba.* Meisenheim am Glan: Verlag Anton Hain.

Goldwater, Robert
    1960   *Bambara Sculpture from the Western Sudan.* New York: The Museum of Primitive Art.

Green, Linda
    1988   Research for a gallery guide. Unpublished copy at University of Iowa Museum of Art.

Griaule, Marcel
    1938   *Masques dogons.* Paris: Institut d'Ethnologie.

de Grunne, Bernard
    1980a   "La Sculpture baTabwa," unpublished M.A. thesis. Louvain: Université Catholique de Louvain. Institut Supérieur d'Archéologie et d'Histoire d'Art.
    1980b   *Terres cuites anciennes de l'ouest africain.* Louvain: Institut Supérieur d'Archéologie et d'Histoire d'Art.

    1981   *Ancient Treasures in Terra Cotta of Mali and Ghana.* New York: The African-American Institute.
    1983   *Ancient Pottery from Mali.* Munich: Fred and Jens Jahn.

Hall, H. U.
    1923   "Baluba Chieftain's staff," *Museum Journal* (University of Pennsylvania) 14(3): 192–197.

Harter, Pierre
    1984   Personal communication.
    1986   *Arts anciens du Cameroun.* Arnouville: Arts d'Afrique Noire.

de Havenon, Gaston
    1971   *African Art: The de Havenon Collection.* Washington, D.C.: The Museum of African Art.

Hersak, Dunja
    1986   *Songye Masks and Figure Sculpture.* London.

de Heusch, Luc
    1972   *Le Roi ivre, ou L'Origine de l'état.* Paris: Gallimard.

Himmelheber, Hans and G. W. Tahmen
    1965   "Wunkirle, die gastliche Frau," *Festschrift Alfred Buhler.* Basel.

Holy, Ladislav
    1967   *Masks and Figures from Eastern and Southern Africa.* London: Paul Hamlyn.

Huber, Hugo
    1956   "Magical Statuettes and their Accessories Among the Eastern Bayaka and Their Neighbors (Belgian Congo)," *Anthropos* 51: 264–290.

Huet, Michel
    1978   *The Dance, Art and Ritual of Africa.* New York: Pantheon.

Imperato, Pascal James
    1984   Personal communication.

Jahn, Fred
    1980   *Colonne Colon Kolo.* Munich: Galerie Fred Jahn.

Jones, G. I.
    1984   *The Art of Eastern Nigeria.* Cambridge: Cambridge University Press.

Jordan, Manuel
    1991   Gallery Guide to the Chokwe Objects in the Stanley Collection. Unpublished copy at University of Iowa Museum of Art.

Kasfir, Sidney
    1979   "The Visual Arts of the Idoma of Central Nigeria," Ph.D. thesis (ms.). London: University of London, School of Oriental and African Studies.
    1984   Personal communication.

Kazadi, Ntole
    1980   "Scarification et langage dans la culture des Bahemba." Unpublished conference paper, University of Pennsylvania.

Kecskési, Maria
    1982   *Kunst aus dem Alten Afrika.* Munich: Staatliches Museum für Völkerkunde.

Kjersmeier, Carl
    1935-38   *Centres de style de la sculpture nègre africaine.* Paris: Albert Morancé.

Krieger, Kurt
    1965   *Westafrikanische Plastik I.* Berlin: Museum für Völkerkunde.

Kuennen-Jordan, Claire
    1983   "The Anthropomorphic Pottery of the Mangbetu of Northeastern Zaire." The University of Iowa, School of Art and Art History. Unpublished M.A. thesis.
    1984   Personal communication.

Laude, Jean
    1973   *African Art of the Dogon.* New York: The Brooklyn Museum.

Lehuard, Raoul
    1977   *Les Phemba du Mayombe.* Arnouville: Arts d'Afrique Noire.
    1980   *Fétiches à clous de Bas-Zaire.* Arnouville: Arts d'Afrique Noire.

Leiris, Michel and Jacqueline Delange
    1968   *African Art.* Arts of Mankind, general editor, André Malraux. New York: Golden Press.

Lem, F. H.
    1948   *Sculptures soudanaises.* Paris: Arts et Métiers Graphiques.

Leurquin, Anne and Georges Meurant
    1990   "Tanzanie méconnue," *Arts d'Afrique Noire* 73: 13–20.

Leuzinger, Elsy
1960   *Africa: The Art of the Negro Peoples*. London: Methuen.
Lips, Julius
1966   *The Savage Hits Back*. New Hyde Park, N.Y.: University Books. Translation of the 1937 German edition.
von Luschan, Felix
1900   "Afrikanische Lehnstühle," *Globus* 77: 259–261.

Maes, Joseph
1929   *Les Appuis tête du Congo Belge*, Tome 1, Part 1. Tervuren: Royal Museum of Central Africa.
1938   *Kabila en Grafbeelden uit Kongo*. Annales du Musée du Congo Belge, series 6, Catalogues des collections ethnographiques du Musée du Congo Belge, vol. 2, part 2. Tervuren: Musée du Congo Belge.
1939a   *Kabila en Grafbeelden uit Kongo—Addenda*. Annales du Musée du Congo Belge, series 6, Catalogues des collections ethnographiques du Musée du Congo Belge, vol. 2, part 3. Tervuren: Musée du Congo Belge.
1939b   *Mooedereerebeelden uit Kongo*. Annales du Musée du Congo Belge, series 6, Catalogues des collections ethnographiques du Musée du Congo Belge, vol. 2, part 3. Tervuren: Musée du Congo Belge.
Maes, Joseph and Olga Boone
1935   *Les Peuplades du Congo Belge*. Brussels: Musée Royal de l'Afrique Centrale, Documentation ethnologique, series 2.
Maesen, Albert
1967   *Art of the Congo*. Minneapolis: Walker Art Center.
1969   *Umbangu: Art du Congo au Musée Royal du Congo Belge*. Tervuren: Musée Royal de l'Afrique Centrale.
1984   Personal communication.
de Mahieu, Wauthier
1935   *Qui a obstrué la cascade? Analyse sémantique du rituel de la circoncision chez les Komo du Zaïre*. Cambridge: Cambridge University Press.
1937   "Danses," *Les Beaux-Arts* 7(227): 18–19.
de Maret, P., N. Dery and C. Murdoch
1973   "The Luba Shankadi Style," *African Arts* 7(1): 8–15.
McIntosh, Roderick J. and Susan K. McIntosh
1979   "Terracotta Statuettes from Mali," *African Arts* 12(2): 51–53.
McLeod, Malcolm
1976   "Verbal Elements in West African Arts," *Quaderni Poro* 1: 85–102.
Merriam, Alan
1974   *An African World*. Bloomington: Indiana University Press.
1978   "Kifwebe and Other Masked and Unmasked Societies Among the Basongye," *Africa-Tervuren* 24.
Messenger, John C.
1973   "The Carver in Anang Society," in *The Traditional Artist in African Societies*, edited by Warren d'Azevedo. Bloomington: Indiana University Press.
Mestach, J. W.
1984   Personal communication.
1985   *Songye Studies: Form and Symbolism*. Munich: Galerie Fred Jahn.
Meyer, Piet
1981   *Kunst und Religion der Lobi*. Zurich: Museum Rietberg.
1984   Personal communication.
Millot, Jacques
1961   "De Pointe-Noire au pays tsogho," *Objets et Mondes* 1(3–4): 65–80.
Moeller, A.
1936   *Les Grandes Lignes des migrations des Bantous de la province orientale du Congo belge*. Brussels: Institut Royal Colonial Belge.
Mudiji-Selenge, Malutshi
1984   Personal communication.
Muensterberger, Warner
1955   *Sculpture of Primitive Man*. New York: Abrams.

Murray, Kenneth C.
1949   *Masks and Headdresses of Nigeria*. London: Zwemmer Gallery.
Newton, Douglas and Lee Bolton
1978   *Masterpieces of Primitive Art*. New York: Knopf.
Neyt, François
1977   *La Grande Statuaire hemba du Zaïre*. Louvain: Institut Supérieur d'Archéologie et d'Histoire de l'Art.
1979   *L'Art eket: Collection Azar*. Paris: Azar.
1981   *Traditional Art and History of Zaire*. Brussels: Société d'Arts Primitifs.
1982   *L'Art holo du Haut-Kwango*. Munich: Fred Jahn.
Nooter, Mary (Polly)
1984a   "The Female Image in Luba Prestige Art." Paper presented at the Frick Symposium on the History of Art, April 7, 1984.
1984b   "Luba Arts and Leadership." Columbia University, unpublished M.A. thesis.
1984c   Personal communication.
1990   "Secret Signs in Luba Sculptural Narrative: A Discourse on Power," *Iowa Studies in African Art* 3: 35–60.
1991   "Luba Art and Government: Creating Power in a Central African Kingdom," Ph.D. dissertation, Department of Art History, Columbia University.
Nooter, Nancy
1989   "High-Backed Stools: A Pan-Ethnic Tradition in East Africa." Unpublished paper presented at the 32nd annual meeting of the African Studies Association, Atlanta.
Northern, Tamara
1984   *The Art of Cameroon*. Washington: Smithsonian Institution.
Olbrechts, Frans
1937   *Tentoonstelling van Kongo-Kunst*. Antwerpsche Propagandaweken.
1959   *Les Arts plastiques du Congo belge*. Brussels: Editions Erasme.
Paulme, Denise
1959   "Elek: A Ritual Sculpture of the Baga of French Guinea," *Man* 59: 28–29.
Pemberton, John
1984   Personal communication.
Perrois, Louis
1972   *La Statuaire fan, Gabon*. Paris: O.R.S.T.O.M.
1977   *La Sculpture traditionnelle du Gabon*. Paris: O.R.S.T.O.M. (Initiations—Documentations Techniques #32).
1979   *Art du Gabon*. Arnouville: Arts d'Afrique Noire.
Redmayne, Alison
1973   "The Hehe," in *Tanzania Before 1900*, ed. Andrew Roberts, 37–58. Nairobi: East African Publishing House.
Reefe, Thomas
1981   *The Rainbow and the Kings*. Berkeley: University of California Press.
Richards, Audrey I.
1935   "Bow-Stand or Trident," *Man* (February) 32.
Roberts, Allen
1985a   "Catalogue of the Exhibition," in Roberts and Maurer 1985, 98–218.
1985b   "Social and Historical Contexts of Tabwa Art," in Roberts and Maurer 1985, 1–45.
1986   "Les Arts du corps chez les Tabwa," *Arts d'Afrique Noire* 59: 15–29.
1988a   "Tabwa Tegumentary Inscription," in *Marks of Civilization: Artistic Transformations of the Human Body*, ed. A. Rubin, 41–56. Los Angeles: UCLA Museum of Cultural History.
1988b   "Through the Bamboo Thicket: The Social Process of Tabwa Ritual Performance," *TDR: The Drama Review* 32(2): 123–138.
1990a   "Tabwa Masks, 'An Old Trick of the Human Race,'" *African Arts* 23(2): 36–47, 101–103.
1990b   "Initiation, Art and Ideology in Southeastern Zaire," *Iowa Studies in African Art* 3: 7–32.
in press "Where the King is Coming From," in *Body, Gender and Space: African Folk Models of Social and Cosmological Order*, ed. Anita Jakobsen-Widding. *Uppsala Studies in Cultural Anthropology*. Stockholm: Almqvist and Wiksell.

Roberts, Allen and Evan Maurer, eds.
1985 *The Rising of a New Moon: A Century of Tabwa Art*. Seattle: University of Washington Press for the University of Michigan Museum.

Roberts, Andrew D.
1973 "The Nyamwezi," in *Tanzania Before 1900*, ed. A. D. Roberts, 117–150. Nairobi: East African Publishing House.

Rogers, Donna
1979 *Royal Art of the Kuba*. Austin: University of Texas Art Museum.

Rosenwald, Jean
1974 "Kuba King Figures," African Arts 7(3): 26–31, 92.

Roy, Christopher D.
1979a *African Sculpture: The Stanley Collection*. Iowa City: The University of Iowa Museum of Art.
1979b *Mossi Masks and Crests*. Ph.D. dissertation, Indiana University. University Microfilms, Ann Arbor, Michigan.
1981 *African Art from Iowa Private Collections*. Iowa City: The University of Iowa Museum of Art.
1987 *Art of the Upper Volta Rivers*. Meudon: Chaffin.

Sassoon, Hamo
1983 "Kings, Cattle and Blacksmiths: Royal Insignia and Religious Symbolism in the Interlacustrine States," *Azania* 18.

Schildkrout, Enid and Curtis A. Keim
1990 *African Reflections: Art from Northeastern Zaire*. New York: American Museum of Natural History.

Schubotz, Dr. H.
1913 "From Fort Archimbault to the Nile," in *From the Congo to the Niger and the Nile*, by Adolf Friedrich. London: Duckworth.

Sendwe, Jason
1955 "Traditions et coutumes ancestrales chez les Baluba shankadji," *Problèmes Sociaux Congolais* 31: 57–84.

Shorter, Aylward
1972 *Chiefship in Western Tanzania*. London: Oxford University Press.

Sieber, Roy
1961 *Sculpture of Northern Nigeria*. New York: The Museum of Primitive Art.
1984 Personal communication.

Siroto, Leon
1972 "*Gon*: A Mask Used in Competition for Leadership Among the Bakwele," *African Art and Leadership*, edited by Douglas Fraser and Herbert M. Cole. Madison: University of Wisconsin Press.

Smith, Andrea L.
1988 Gallery guide. Unpublished copy at University of Iowa Museum of Art.

de Sousberghe, Leon
1958 *L'Art pende*. Brussels: Académie Royale de Belgique.

Speke, James Hanning
1863 *Journey of Discovery of the Sources of the Nile*. New York: Harper Brothers.

Stanley, Henry Morton
1890 *In Darkest Africa*. London.

Stoll, Mareidi and Gert Stoll
1980 *Ibeji: Twin Figures of the Yoruba*. Munich: Stoll.

Swantz, Marja-Liisa
1970 *Ritual and Symbolism in Transitional Zaramo Society: With Special Reference to Women*. Uppsala: Scandinavian Institute of African Studies.

von Sydow, Eckart
1932 *Kunst der Naturvölker*. Berlin: Cassirer.

Tatum, Steven
1984 "Luba Sculpture in the Stanley Collection." Iowa City: University of Iowa, School of Art and Art History. M.A. Thesis.

Theuws, Theodore
1962 *De Luba-Mens*. Tervuren: MRAC, Série Sciences Humaines 38.

Thompson, Robert Farris
1970 "The Sign of the Divine King: An Essay on Yoruba Bead-Embroidered Crowns with Veil and Bird Decorations," *African Arts* 3(3): 8–17, 74–80.
1978 "The Grand Detroit N'kondi," *Bulletin of the Detroit Institute of Arts* 56(4): 206–221.

Timmermans, Paul
1966 "Essai de typologie de la sculpture des Bena Luluwa du Kasai," *Africa Tervuren* 12(1): 17–27.
1967 "Les Lwalwa," *Africa Tervuren* 13(3–4): 73–90.

Torday, Emil
1925 *On the Trail of the Bushongo*. London: Seeley, Service and Co.

Torday Emil and Thomas Athol Joyce
1910 *Notes ethnographiques sur les peuples communement appelés Bakuba ainsi que sur les peuplades apparentées les Bushongo*. Brussels: Ministère des Colonies.

Trowel, Margaret (with Ferdinand Anton, Frederick Dockstader, and Hans Neverman)
1979 *Primitive Art*. New York: Abrams.

Van Avermaet, Ernest
1954 *Dictionnaire kiluba-français*. Tervuren: MRCB, Série Sciences de l'Homme, Linguistique 7.

Vandergam, H.
1930 "Sectes secrètes: Wagabo," unpublished administrative report from Kabalo, dated 30 July. Kalemie, Zaire: Archives of the district of Tanganyika.

Van Geertruyen, Godelieve
1976 "La Fonction de la sculpture dans une société africaine: les Baga, Nalu et Landuman," *Africana Gandensia Gent* 1: 63–117.
1979 "Le Style nimba," *Arts d'Afrique Noire* 31: 20–37.

Van Geluwe, Huguette
1978 "Half-Bell-Shaped Mask 'Mvondo,'" *Vingt-cinq sculptures africaines*, Jacqueline Fry, editor. Ottawa: National Museums of Canada.

Van Malderen, A.
1936 "Organisation politique et judiciaire coutumières de la chefferie de Mufunga (territoire de Sampwe—district du Haut-Katanga)" . . . *Bulletin des Juridictions et du Droit Coutumier Congolais* 4(9): 174–178.

Vansina, Jan
1960 "Recording the Oral History of the Bakuba, 2. Results," *Journal of African History* 1(2): 257–270.
1966 *Introduction à l'ethnographie du Congo belge*. Kinshasa: Éditions Universitaires du Congo.
1978 *The Children of Woot: A History of the Kuba Peoples*. Madison: University of Wisconsin Press.

Van Vyve, G.
1927 "Secte des Bagabo," unpublished administrative report from Kilunga dated 1 November. Kalemie, Zaire: Archives of the district of Tanganyika.

Vatter, Ernst
1926 *Religiose Plastik der Naturvölker*. Frankfurt: Frankfurter Verlags-Anstalt.

Vergiat, A. M.
1937 *Moeurs et coutumes des Manjas*. Paris.

Verhulpen, Edmond
1936 *Baluba et Balubaises du Katanga*. Anvers.

Vogel, Susan Mullen
1973 "People of Wood: Baule Figure Sculpture," *The Art Journal* 33(1): 23–26.
1977 *Baule Art as an Expression of World View*. Ph.D. thesis, New York University. Ann Arbor: University Microfilms International.
1981 *For Spirits and Kings: African Art from the Paul and Ruth Tishman Collection*. New York: The Metropolitan Museum of Art.

Wardwell, Allen
1966 "Some Notes on a Substyle of the Bambara," *Museum Studies* (Chicago Art Institute) 1: 112–128.

Weinrich, Kathryn H.
1988 Gallery guide. Unpublished copy at University of Iowa Museum of Art.

Wescott, Joan
1962 "The Sculpture and Myths of Eshu-Elegba, the Yoruba Trickster: Definition and Interpretation in Yoruba Iconography," *Africa* 32(4): 336–353.

Weule, Karl
1908 "Wissenschaftliche Ergebnisse meiner ethnographischen Forschungsreise in den Südosten Deutsch-Ostafrikas," *Mitteilungen aus den Deutschen Schutzgebiete*, Ergänzungsheft Band I.

1909   *Native Life in East Africa: The Results of an Ethnologic Research Expedition.* New York: D. Appleton.

Weydert, Jean J.
1938   *Les Baluba chez eux.* Heffingen.

White Fathers
1889–1900 "Diaire de la mission de Mpala." Typescript copy in the archives of the Kalemie-Moba Diocese in Kalemie, Zaire (original at the central archives of the Society of African Missioners, Rome).

Williams, Dennis
1974   *Icon and Image: A Study of Sacred and Secular Forms In African Classical Art.* New York: New York University Press.

Witte, Hans
1984   *Ifa and Esu: Iconography of Order and Disorder.* Soest, Holland: Kunsthandel Luttik.

Womersley, Harold
1984   *Legends and History of the Luba.* African Primary Texts, David Henige, editor. Los Angeles: Crossroads Press.

Zahan, Dominique
1975   "Colors and Body Painting in Black Africa," *Diogenes* 90: 100–119.

INDEX